LIMITED ACCESS

CONTENT

INTRODUCTION 1

CHAPTER 1: FOR HIS GLORY 8

CHAPTER 2: THE GREAT SIGHT 24

CHAPTER 3: CONCEIVING THE VISION 41

CHAPTER 4: GET RID OF SUCCESS CLUTTERS 58

CHAPTER 5: BIRTHING YOUR VISION 77

CHAPTER 6: BY WISDOM 94

CHAPTER 7: STICK WITH YOUR TESTED WEAPON 110

CHAPTER 8: THERE IS MORE 128

CHAPTER 9: IN PURSUIT OF EXCELLENCE 146

CHAPTER 10: THE LEGACY 164

FINAL NOTE 176

BOOK SUMMARY 181

INTRODUCTION

Everyone, at one point or the other, has wondered what the future holds and wish they knew all that lies ahead: our untold TOMORROW. Physically speaking, an average human being is limited in sight. It's scientifically proven that an average human being can see the flicker of a candle flame from 30 miles away. But with no definite flicker afar off, the farthest an average person can see is 3 miles away.

I believe it's this intrinsic limitation and desire to know what beauties or horrors lie beyond what we could see with our naked eyes that birthed the invention of Telescope by Hans Lipperhey in the early 1600s. A telescope is an optical tool used to make distanced objects appear closer and clearer. It's an instrument made to aid vision, sight, and clarity.

Here is the beautiful thing: despite not knowing fully what lies ahead of us, we have several telescopic terms we use for managing our fear of the unknown. Some of such terms are: hope, aspiration, dream, ambition, desire, goal, vision and many more. These words seem to manage man's fear of the unknown until we are faced with real-life challenges.

Meanwhile, the Christian has more reliable telescopic tools to capture what lies in the future for him. Some of these tools are God's word, His promises, and what I call a '**God-given vision'.** Hence, the Christian's hope isn't mere optimism. It's security in the infallibility of God and His promises.

Vision is such a powerful tool for navigating your way through life! It deals with confusion. Conceiving and executing a vision is similar to what an architect does. An architect is trained and licensed to plan and design buildings. He creatively draws a blueprint that walks his client from nothing to the completion of a building project.

An architect, before the first block is ever lifted and laid on site, already has the grand design of the house—knowing how it would look like. Whatever a builder or a contractor does on site is simply to bring to reality the vision of the architect.

Vision is to clearly catch a glimpse of the reason for your existence on definite terms. It's the awareness of your God-given assignment. When vision is known, efforts become more concentrated and labors, more rewarding. Vision is the ability to see into the future and the invisible and believe it is possible. Vision is foresight; a peep into tomorrow in the NOW!

Brian Tracy once said, "A clear vision backed by definite plans, gives you tremendous feeling of confidence and personal power." Yet, as powerful and important as vision is, not many people know how to conceive one and execute it in a grand style. Many are the eyes that look; few are the minds that observe. Sadly, our world is full of opened eyes but closed minds.

Hence, in the school of success, physical sight isn't a prime ingredient and an advantage. Every impact a man leaves upon the sands of time and the legacy he lives behind rest on the strength of his vision and how well he's able to execute it. Everything rises and falls on the articulation of your vision for life.

There's a verse in the scriptures that always rattles me whenever I think about the power of vision in the life of a man. The verse reads, *"Where there is no vision, the people perish..."* Proverbs 29:18 (KJV). Can you believe that? Think about what the verse says happens when vision isn't known. The absence of vision is a sure way to sponsor wastage. People go wild when vision isn't in view. And nothing intentional could ever be done without a clear sense of vision.

Why did I say that? The reason is because what you see is what defines what you muster courage to endure in your today. The reason Joseph never slept with Potiphar's wife wasn't because he lost his emotion and feelings as a man. It wasn't even because there was someone around who would let out the secret. The young man had the picture of a majestic future in his mind that he couldn't let go for few minutes of pleasure like

Samson. He could scale through every trap of destruction because he saw something bigger in his vision than a little lap to put his head upon.

In the same vein, Jesus bore the horror and agony of the cross because of the joy He saw ahead of Him. So, when you see a promising young man get stuck while growing up and gets sidetracked into demeaning escapades, why do you think that happened? No clear vision for living; that's why! Your vision, therefore, is that foundation that sustains the entire superstructure of your life. Without a clear vision, you'll lack direction and executing power for life!

Think about how vision played out in God's creation of man. *"And God said, Let us make man in our image, after our likeness: and let them have dominion over the fish of the sea, and over the fowl of the air, and over the cattle, and over all the earth, and over every creeping thing that creepeth upon the earth." Genesis 1:26 (KJV).* Before man was created he was first God's desire and intent! Before the making, there was a clear identification of what God wanted—man!

Notice! The vision was the making of man. It was only after this vision was captured that God set forth the mission statement: **in our image and likeness!** Vision is so powerful that it literarily brings you to the end of your desire and blesses you with the necessary tools for actualization. Man didn't just appear. The first step God took in the creation of man is the conceptualization of what exactly He wanted and what its functions would be.

Here is the actualization: *"So God created man in his own image, in the image of God created he him; male and female created he them." Genesis 1:27 (KJV)* Think about that. God first conceived you in His mind before creating and charging you to have dominion over the cosmic slate—earth. He created exactly what He already captured in His mind. The whole creation is a product of God's grand vision, graphic projection, and design.

There can be no functional mechanism without an agency that defines its workability. God is the ultimate agency behind the emergence of everything created! Man and everything in creation is the fulfilment or actualization of God's desire and intent.

One striking reason for writing this book isn't just to talk about vision but to help you **limit access** to the room where you birth your vision—surrounding yourself with "vision-midwives" and refraining from wasting time with people who will talk you down and make your vision look impossible!

In verse 26 of Genesis one, even though God had the vision to make man, there was a call for partnership *"let us…"* This goes to show that God's creation resulted from **Limited Access.** God knew exactly those He could sell the vision to make man to! It is theologically believed that God the Father, in partnership with the Son and the Holy Spirit were in that birthing room of creation. Not every Dick and Harry deserves your attention at this point.

Many times, we want to bring just anybody on board and make them share and appreciate our vision. Meanwhile, in the birthing room of vision, **Little Access** must be given to anyone who isn't going to help midwife your vision and motivate you to do better. When you allow lots of person in your birthing room, what you get is unprecedented problems and heartaches. You can and should **Limit Access** to your inner circle of vision execution! Jesus doesn't need more than 12 disciples to turn the world upside down.

You must realize that not everyone is interested in your success story or even willing to be a part of it. To force people into supporting your vision is like leaving a gap in the foundation of your vision superstructure. It will cause a terrible collapse in times to come. The Bible said something about Jesus that *"While Jesus was in Jerusalem during the Passover Festival, many believed in him as they saw the miracles he performed.* **But Jesus did not trust himself to them***, because he knew them all. There was no need for anyone to tell him about them, because he himself knew what was in their hearts."* John 2:23-25 (GNB)

Why would Jesus not commit Himself to men who went above the board of unbelief to believing in Him? Was there something Jesus saw in them that made Him pull out from them? Yes!

Let's see why Jesus will not bring many into His birthing room of trust. *"He knew what was in their heart."* Wow! This is powerful. It takes spirit-energized perception to know those worthy of your trust and committal. On the physical plane, those men seemed to have believed in Jesus' vision of glory. But Jesus saw deeper into their hearts.

In fact, there were those who never saw the transfiguration of Jesus among the disciples—just three of them saw the revealed Son in the glory and brightness of His person. To set out to impress everybody with the beauties and brightness of your vision isn't wise. No woman gives birth in the market scene; she's taken into the closet where access is limited to her. You cannot have access to her if you aren't a midwife! You've got to shut the door to gainsayers and make your boundaries stronger against anything that isn't going to help deepen your vision. The multitude can come after the child has broken through every limiting hurdles.

Hence, it's not just enough to conceive a vision; you must understand what it takes to birth your vision and become successful in your field. Through this book, I will usher you into the hub of greatness and success, grant you the keys to a world of endless possibilities, and spur in you a desire to become a generational blessing by the revelation of God's truth.

Let's get started!

CHAPTER 1

FOR HIS GLORY

"You are worthy, O Lord, to receive glory and honor and power; for you created all things, and by your will they exist and were created."

- Revelation 4:11

When you consider nature and its beauties, you'll wonder what God's intent was for making such beauty. Think about the billions of stars in the Milky Way galaxy, the beauties the flowers are adorned with, and the intelligence that rules the wild. It gets more interesting when you realize that just one star is bigger than the earth. I mean, what vastness! If men on earth were to live on a star each, there would still be billions of stars that would not be inhabited.

Aside from the vastness of nature, another thing that baffles me is the uniqueness of every creature. There are no two things in nature that does the same thing and look the same way. As similar as the beet is to the onion, they are still so different from each other. Anyone could confuse a Falcon for an Eagle, but they are still different. As close as the moon sets to the stars on a starry night, they still have different functions. As similar as a bee is to a hornet, they are still unique from each other.

It's wonderful that nature allows each creature to evolve on its own and sustain itself. The vastness, wonder, and uniqueness of nature only points to the fact that it's not design just to be inhabited; it's designed to glorify God—the maker—and reflect His grandeur.

It seemed like the architect of nature—God—planned every creature to be a masterpiece on its own. Seeing the perfection of the Niagara Falls, the bemusing wonder of the Grand Canyon and the beauty of the ice glaciers, one can only bow in reverent awe to God's glory and perfection.

It seems to me like nature is a catalog of designs created and collected by a master designer for His pleasure, as revealed in Revelation 4:11. The true potential of everything God created begins from this basic understanding that *I am fashioned to bring God pleasure AND glory.* You must understand that life itself is a trust and should be lived for the great satisfaction of God.

Just like no one can ever fully operate a device without recourse to the manual made by the manufacturer, man's life would be "under-lived" if we don't see life from God's perspective. From the designer's perspective, to fully function and express all my hidden potentials, I MUST take my tangent from Him.

However, growing up in a society where liberty is pivotal, I have understood that most people believe that their lives belong to them and that they can live it anyhow. That, to me, seems blasphemous. I mean, how will you feel when you see a Porsche own itself and drive itself around? Although there are driverless cars these days, they still have owners. That's just how our world works; nobody is without ownership. We are all owned by someone.

While God is the manufacturer of our lives, He has given us the liberty to choose who we sell ourselves out to. The only liberty you have as an individual is the liberty to choose whom you sell yourself to. You are like a Tesla: intelligent, beautiful, in vogue, and even more, but your owner determines the extent to which your potentials will be harvested.

Some people buy a Tesla just to show off. After buying it, they park it in their oversized garage of other cars. At the same time, others buy the car and start using it functionally while exploring its many features. I'd like you to answer these questions at this point in time: Who owns me? To Whom have I sold myself? Is it to God, to the devil, to other men, to ambitions, or to self?

Well, a Christian is someone who has been redeemed and bought from darkness into God's everlasting light. A Christian is a pilgrim who started off his journey facing Babylon till the grace of God came and created a detour to Zion. So, if you are genuinely born again, and have received the life of Christ into you, then you should continue with me as I take you on a journey to getting more out of life.

But if you are yet to open the door of your heart to Jesus, I would advise you to pause at this point and consider your life. Life is more than what you conceive it to be. Let the designer of your life take you through the journey of your life. Then, I would suggest you continue this book after you've decided to allow God to pilot your life. Do you want to experience what it is to be MORE? Allow God into your heart now!

Having said this, I must mention that there is a deception that most Christians have fallen into. This is a pitfall you must be careful of if you will live your life in line with God's divine plans and purposes. That deception, is seeking self-discovery outside the person of God. It is appalling that man seeks to discover an image of himself that does not align with His maker.

Let's see how man was made in Genesis 1.:26, The Bible records it this way: "Then God said, "*Let Us make man in Our image, according to Our likeness; let them have dominion over the fish of the sea, over the birds of the air, and over the cattle, over all the earth and over every creeping thing that creeps on the earth."* Did you see that?

The design of man was modeled after none but God. Man is an image of God and a reflection of His divine nature. The easiest way to see it is this: when God looks in a mirror, He sees man! And when a man looks into the mirror, he should see God because he was designed to express the image of God. When nature looks for God in the earth realm, it should make recourse to man.

But then, what has gone wrong? How come man is living way below what he was made to be. Man has become like a Rolls-Royce that operates like a Volkswagen Beetle. What a depreciation! The cause of this problem is not far-fetched. Man is so obsessed with self-discovery that he does not find who he has been made to be.

The way most people run after self, you would think they made themselves and everything in their lives belong to them. What most of them do is leave themselves behind and start searching for what they hope to see as themselves. How can someone God made as a beautiful young man discover himself as a lady restricted by his male organs?

It's high time Man stopped seeking self-discovery and moved higher into the only one that can make him know who he is. That is God. Man was modeled after God; the more man understands and experiences God, the more of himself he finds. So it's time we stopped going after self-discovery and started God-discovery.

GOD-DISCOVERY

Before I tell you what I mean by God-discovery, let me first give you a little more insight into the word I coined it from—self-discovery. According to Merriam Webster's dictionary, self-discovery is the act or process of achieving self-knowledge. In other words, it is when a person comes to understand things about themselves that would help them maximize their potentials.

In the same vein, God-discovery is the process or act of achieving God-knowledge. It is simply when a man comes into the understanding of who God made him to be and how to access the many blessings God has encoded into him. It is the opening of a man's understanding to the many blessings God has imputed into his being. What then are these things?

At this point, it is essential that I reiterate to you this important fact—you can only discover what God has made you become as you discover Him. This implies that God-discovery is not you using God as a means to find yourself; instead, you see yourself as you see God. Simply put, you've come to the realization that you were created in God's image, and the more of God you see, the more His life rubs on you and you start living the way He designed you to be.

In Genesis 1:26, after God commanded that man be made in His image, he mentioned his mandate. "That he might have dominion..." dominion is not servitude, neither is it shared ownership; it is supremacy! So when God made man, He gave him the mandate to function as He does. To dominate everything just like God does.

HOW THEN CAN A MAN FIND GOD?

> *"And you will seek Me and find Me when you search for Me with all your heart."*
> - Jeremiah 29: 13

The first step to finding God is that the pursuit of God is done wholeheartedly. You can't get the whole of God when you seek Him with half your heart. So when you seek God in the place of prayer, worship, or Bible study, it's is essential the whole of your heart is hinged on finding nothing else but God.

This is how our prayers as Christians have become tools of self-propagation. We find what we want and then pressure God into our will through prayer. This will never work. If you will find God and ultimately discover what He has made you be, then it must be done with the totality of your being. With the whole of your heart and the whole of your mind. God cannot be mocked because while men look at your efforts, God weighs your heart.

Another problem people have with their hearts is inconsistency. They seek God truly and deeply for a season, and when they get what they want for that time or if it seems like answers are not coming, they abandon God and start consulting their plan. At times, some individuals make God plan B. They first try what they planned; when it fails, they run to God for help. They've forgotten that for God to be the finisher of a thing, He must have authored it. He is the author first before He is the finisher.

What is that thing in your life that God has not authored? He definitely won't finish it. So instead of making mistakes and asking God to help you, why not get the God perspective and work with it. Instead of trying out many options first and now running to God when they fail, why not get your options from Him and set your life in the course based on His instruction and guidance. This is easier and ultimately more beneficial to you.

The Bible says, *"I love those who love me, and those who seek me early and diligently shall find me."* Proverbs 8:17. And there you have another vital point to consider in God-discovery—timing. God says in this portion of the Bible that He loves those who love Him, but it's only those that seek Him early that find Him. This is a profound mystery you must understand in life to make a breakthrough in your pursuit of

God. Therefore, it is essential you seek God early for Him to be found. The question that arises then is this: when is early?

The idea of seeking God early can be fit into several contexts. The first of these contexts is a man's life. The Bible says in Ecclesiastes 12:1 that "you should remember your Creator in the days of your youth when the evil day hasn't come"; you must start seeking God early in life. This will give you a head start and help you avoid unnecessary problems and troubles. A man that starts seeking God early in life has more chances of discovering his God-given purpose and walking in it before making severe errors.

If you consider men that God used tremendously in the Bible and in our present times, most of them started with Him early in life. While they were choosing their careers, locations, marriages, and life goals, God was there instructing them and guiding them. For example, David had been in the Wilderness with God before the Bible began recording anything about him.

Joseph, Daniel, Moses, Jesus; these men had been following God since they were young. They had already been accustomed to the voice, the will, and the ways of God. Hence, it was easy for them to find themselves in the light of who God designed them to be. They were men who already knew what God would have them do, and they only sought to walk in the path He had laid before them because they already knew it.

Another context of seeking God early is when we seek him in the early hours of the day. This is a secret to help increase the efficacy of our devotion and meditation on God's word. In Mark 1:35, the Bible mentioned how Jesus Christ woke up "a great while before day" and went to fellowship with God.

Given that life is lived in sections. Days birth weeks; weeks birth months; months birth years; and years birth a lifetime. Starting every day with fellowship with God will go a long way in helping you discover Him. That will ultimately help you live in the NOW. You will know what God will have you do per day, which will ultimately guide you to live a life that God guides.

The final context of seeking God early involves Him at the beginning of our plans. The rate at which Christians make avoidable mistakes is alarming! This is so because we usually think we've got things under control till they go out of control. God is not just an antidote for healing failures and mistakes. He wants to help you prevent it.

Instead of resorting to God when your plans no longer work, why not start by going to Him for a plan? When He gives you a plan, He adds detail and tells you when to do what and where. His guidance is never ambiguous, and He wants to lead you into all truths and beautiful things. He wants to be more than the Lord of your ending; He wants to be the end of your beginning. Remember, He is not Lord at all if He is not Lord of all.

You were designed for His glory. Why do you seek to live for your own glory? No man can adequately live for God's glory if he doesn't allow God to help him live. No man can live the life of glory and virtue that God has called him to if he does not find God first. Dump the quest for self-discovery and take on the quest for God-discovery. When you find God, you find all you need for life.

THE VISION, THE PURPOSE, AND THE GLORY

"I will say to the north, 'Give them up!' And to the south, 'Do not keep them back!' Bring My sons from afar, And My daughters from the ends of the earth—Everyone who is called by My name, Whom I have created for My glory; I have formed him, yes, I have made him."

- Isaiah 43:6-7

In the Bible verse quoted above, God reveals a transformational secret to you and me. That secret is the secret of man's functionality. It says that "everyone who is called in God's name who he has created for his glory..." God did not design man to give glory to another or himself but that his name might be glorified.

You'll remember that during creation, man was reserved till the last day. God had created everything, and he was already glorified, but it seems like there needed to be an extension of His person in this realm that had just been created. It seemed like God needed a creature that had his nature in Him, who would show forth the fullness of God's glory.

Man was created as the seal of God's glory. He was the last creature that was supposed to have dominion over all others. He was to keep the earth radiating in God's glory. That is why God gave him the commandment to till the garden and tend to it. By tending to it and keeping it, he maintained order and kept watch to ensure that everything radiates God's glory.

In short, man was made primarily to show forth God's glory. Interestingly, he was formed not only to be a reflection of the glory and splendour of God, but he was also made to keep the glory of God hosted on earth. This duty is meant to be fulfilled in two ways. First, by expressing the 'glory' nature of God that he had internalized. Second, by bringing down the glory of God to this realm through fellowship and communion.

Let's take a peek at the relationship Adam had with God in the Garden of Eden before sin entered. After God made him in his image and likeness and gave him his job description, he asked him to express one of the only things humans share with God: creativity! God brought everything he had made to the extension of His glory, and because Adam sustained the glory of God internally, he was able to give them names that glorified God. Thus fulfilling the first expression of God's glory in him.

Furthermore, the Bible records that God typically comes to Adam and his wife in the cool of the day. This is a show of how much of God's glory Adam handled. After possessing the 'glory' nature through the image of God in him, he also renews the glory and increases it by a consistent encounter with God. It was in the cool of the day when he was away from all the bustles and activities around.

Having seen the original pattern God made you should be challenged to ask this question: what has gone wrong? Seeing that God infused the nature of 'glory' into us through his image in us, and he seeks to increase it through fellowship, why then do our lives seem so void of God's glory? I mean, why are the sons of God so destitute of the revelation and reality of His glory?

This book will answer these questions deeply in its chapters. It will run you through the depths of how your life can fully radiate the glory of God. Although this book is designed to take you intensely into how the vision you get about your purpose for God can help you access the glory of God and house it, this portion of the book will introduce you to how vision, purpose, and glory are interrelated.

According to Dr. Myles Munroe, "*Purpose is when you know and understand what you were born to accomplish; vision is when you see it in your mind and begin to imagine it.*" The first step to living the fullness of God's life before you is seeking Him till you find your purpose. Finding one's purpose in God is not spontaneous. You have to invest your prayers, profound studies, and alignment.

To find your God-given purpose is to go into God's word and prayerfully wait on Him till you get accustomed to his reassuring voice. A man that has not learned to hear God clearly for himself will find it difficult to download what his purpose is in God. It's only in His presence that the reason for your existence can be revealed.

Like I said earlier, the more of God you discover, the more of your Self you find. God has the reality of your person in His divine wisdom. What then is your purpose? This question will only be answered as you continue seeking God. The Bible says He is a reward for them that diligently seek Him. Whether or not it seems like it is making sense, continue seeking God till He reveals to you what your purpose is.

After discovering your purpose, however, you'll need to translate it into a vision. A purpose is a knowing, a consciousness of what you are designed to be by God, while a vision is a revelation of where you are going alongside all the things you'll have to do to get there. Your knowledge of what you are designed to be is your purpose, while your revelation of how to get there is your vision. The destination you hope to get to is what we can tag as glory.

Translating one's purpose into vision is not something that can happen arbitrarily; some steps must be taken to achieve this. I would run you through some of these steps subsequently.

1. Stay focused on your purpose: while knowledge can be tagged as purpose, vision must be graphic; that is, it must be one you can picture and capture with the eye of your mind. Hence, it would be best if you learned to focus on your purpose till your mind can conceive a picture of it. It is not enough to wish your dreams come true; you have to stay focused on it, understand it is your purpose, and you have to achieve it.

This focus level will help it burn into your mind, and before you know it, the knowledge of your purpose gradually becomes a vision that drives you towards the expression of God's glory that you have been called unto. Of course, there is a nature of glory in you, but you will find it difficult to express this nature and show forth God's glory if you do not learn to stay on what God has called you into, then translate it to a vision that your life is patterned to achieve.

2. Believe in your purpose: there are times when it will seem like what God said about you is a lie. The situations that will be obtainable in your life might make it difficult for you to keep on trusting and waiting on God. This is why God commanded in the book of Habakkuk 2:1-2 that you should "write the vision down and make it plain upon the tables..." When your vision is written and sealed, you understand that there is no plan B. It is either it works, or you do not work!

Knowing this, you will learn to wait on God and trust his capabilities over your life. When God speaks to you about your life, He does not do so to make you scared or unsecured; He speaks that you might receive life and learn to bring forth the life He has called you into. When you believe in the purpose God has called you into, you will be able to translate it to visualize and ultimately glorify Him by realizing it.

3. Let God help you all the way: this can never be overemphasized. Man was not designed to survive outside the person of God. Remember, he is an image of God, more like a reflection. It takes an original for a reflection to be sensible. The sensibility of your life can only be found in the person of God. So as you seek to discover what you are made to be, do not forget that it has been hidden in God, and the more of God you see, the more of yourself you find.

CHAPTER 2

THE GREAT SIGHT

"And Moses said, I will now turn aside and see this great sight, why the bush is not burned."

- Exodus 3:3

Human beings have five sense organs, that is; there are five organs in the human body that connect us with external things and sensations. There is the sense of feeling, of taste, of smelling and of sight. Of all these senses, however; the sense of sight is one of the most important. Sight is the only sense organ that connects man to light; it is one of the organs needed to access God.

Given that light is God's medium of communication, sight is imperative in receiving instructions from God. While men communicate with words and actions, God communicates with light! Whenever God speaks, he communicates light and clarity, hence it is important that a Christian's organ of sight is sharp to receive from God.

In the Bible verse quoted above, Moses had a sensitive sight that was able to see what an ordinary man would not have seen. That sight was not just an unusual occurrence that Moses ran into, it was an encounter that defined his life and ministry from that point onwards. What would have happened if he hadn't seen the bush?

We might never had heard of Moses' ministry ever again. That little time of going up to see what seemed out of the ordinary. How many of us have lost destiny transforming encounters because we failed to see? How many times we have lost touch with divine arrangements because our sight wasn't sharp enough to access God's provision?

The Bible says in Habakkuk 2:1 (AMP) that "OH, I know, I have been rash to talk out plainly this way to God!] I will [in my thinking stand upon my post of observation and station myself on the tower or fortress, and will watch to see what He will say within me and what answer I will make [as His mouthpiece] to the perplexities of my complaint against Him." It says that I will stand on my post of observation; instead of rushing to speak, what you are supposed to do is to sit and watch.

What baffles me is that Habakkuk says he will watch to see what would be said to Him. This shows that the word of God is not just a book to be read but a sight to be beheld. No wonder the Bible says that as we behold the word of God as in atlas we become transformed into his image. The sense of sight is important in getting from God. This is why it is important that like Moses you decide to step up to see this great sight that only God offers.

However most people refuse to go up to God that they might see. This is so because people tend to think they've got things in control. But if you will get help from Him, that will benefit your present and future. It is important you learn to see the great sight that God is offering in every facets of your life.

Do you know that most people grew up having never learnt how to bathe or the proper way to brush their teeth because they think these are normal everyday things? But this is not necessarily true, the fact that they are everyday things do not mean that there is not a right way to do them. You just need to see better ways to do them to your own benefit.

What do I mean? I mean, someone could keep brushing their teeth with a stiff brush and think it actually does them good because there is no immediate repercussion; they think it is the right thing to do. However, when their dental health starts deteriorating, and the enamel is injured, it'll be almost too late to remediate the situation.

An average human being thinks they're in charge till they actually lose control. You will agree with me that man did not design himself. You did not make yourself, and in the preceding chapter, I have introduced you to the fact that God made you for His glory. I have shown you that it is important you catch a glimpse of your purpose and translate it to a vision to live a life that glorifies God.

If you do not allow God to reveal it to you, you may never know the right things to fit into your life. Except God Himself reveals it, there are potentials and valuables that He has kept in you to help you show forth His glory, but you will never know them or use them if you do not seek His help. He is the maker of mysteries and the revealer of secrets. You are a mystery made by Gift waiting to be revealed when you seek Him.

However, over the ages, there has been a consistent pattern through which God brings men to understand and walk in His purpose for their lives. This pattern is a system through which God deliberately draws a man to walk in the plane and purposes He has for such a life. We would see the steps in this pattern and how God uses each step of the pattern to bring a man to know and walk in His purposes.

GOD'S PATTERN FOR PURPOSE DISCOVERY

"Who has saved us and called us with a holy calling, not according to our works, but according to His own purpose and grace which was given to us in Christ Jesus before time began."

- 2 Timothy 1:9

The pattern through which God engages men and reveals the purpose He has for them starts at salvation. In the Bible verse above, the Bible says, "who has saved us and called us with a holy calling..." God did not call people He hasn't saved. He saves first before calling.

In the plan of God for man, salvation is the gate. It is the point that gives access to a Christian in every facet of life. Salvation opens a man up to the realities that exist in God. in other words, salvation introduces a man to God. At salvation, we are called to what God has made us for; this is His divine purpose.

Have you accepted the finished work of Christ? Have you been saved by the grace that comes through Christ Jesus? The Bible says there is no other name under heaven given among by which we must be saved. So it is not your good heart that saves you, neither is it your longing; it is your surrender to the finished works of Christ on the cross.

God has a plan in His mind that every man must execute before he is made. However, due to the fallen nature of sin that works in every man who has not been saved, it becomes difficult for man to know or walk in the purpose of God. This is why the first step towards knowing your purpose of salvation. Every man who has not embraced the saving grace of Christ is blind to God's glory and His grace.

Furthermore, the Bible says in 2 Timothy 3:16-17 that *"All Scripture is given by inspiration of God, and is profitable for doctrine, for reproof, for correction, for instruction in righteousness, that the man of God may be complete, thoroughly equipped for every good work."* The next step in the pattern of God for revealing His purpose to men is sound doctrine.

You see, God's purpose is so perfect and impeccable that when a man knows it, he might be tempted to want to jump processes and disrespect authorities. This is where doctrine comes in. Doctrine is the body of preparatory lesson and teaching that equips a man for his destiny. If you would go far in what God has called you into, you first must learn to sit and learn doctrine.

When He seeks to bring you to work in His ways, God starts exposing you to the quality doctrine that can build you up. God deliberately puts you in a place where you, like a grain of wheat, can fall to the ground and die first. God knows that if you fulfill

His purpose for your life, then your ego, will, and ambitions must die first.

Hence, He connects you to a source you can draw life from, a source where you learn the pros and cons of His kingdom from. When God seeks to make a man walk in purpose, He doesn't reveal his purpose to him first; He reveals Christ to him first. Therefore, your God-given purpose can only be found in the knowledge of Christ.

Before God works through a man, He first works in that man. He will never send a man He has not prepared: teachings, mentorship, and discipleship are God's methods for building lives into what He wants. He will not use a son that has not learned sonship, nor will he use a daughter that is yet to be polished according to the similitude of the palace.

Interestingly, the Bible says in Romans 8: 28 that "*all things work together for good to them that love God, to those; who are the called according to His purpose.*" Another vital step through which God draws men to live the life He has called them unto these situations. God uses situations and happenings around to point men to Him.

He permits hardships and difficulties to work as the fire through which His servants emerge as gold. While God is good and His mercies endure forever, He allows his children to go through situations that will make them into what He wants. He does not only lead us through the still waters, but also the valley of the shadows of death.

There are times in life when it'll seem like nothing is making sense; these are times when we'll look around and see that where we expected help from, help seems to be veering far away. But, this is not a time to cave away under pressure or a time to give up on your dreams; it is a time to keep on trusting God, knowing that He's got all things in control.

The Bible shows the relationship between hardship and development in a Christian's life in the book of Romans 5:3-5, *"And not only that but we also glory in tribulations, knowing that tribulation produces perseverance; and perseverance, character; and character, hope. Now hope does not disappoint because the love of God has been poured out in our hearts by the Holy Spirit who was given to us."*

Did you see that? Tribulations produce perseverance; this is true because you learn to trust God through it when you are faced with tribulations. Hence focusing your gaze on God. It is easy for anyone to say they'll hold on to God's will and His ways, but it is tribulations and situations that try a man's decision and teaches him to wait on God.

Furthermore, perseverance forms character, and character forms hope. But, unfortunately, our generation is characterized by many Christians who do not have characters that can attract men to the simplicity of Christ's nature. Well, this is so because most Christians today take the easy way out. They do not allow God to help them through situations where they might learn patience, character, and hope.

Most Christians resort to self-help therapies, psychological advice, and the wisdom of men as a substitute for the divine wisdom taught by God's sacred word. But then, just like the Bible says: God cannot be mocked; whatever pattern you fit yourself into is what you will turn out to be. So when you are faced with situations that seem overwhelming, don't cave under pressure or chicken out. Instead, simply wait on God till He helps you. That situation is working out God's plan in you.

Having said that, it is needful that I expose to you how God grants sight to men. You see, different men come to God and find out different things. It was the same God that gave Samson strength that gave Solomon wisdom. The same God gave Moses a burden for the Israelites in captivity that inspired Nehemiah to rebuild the walls.

There are things that would look ordinary to some people but the Lord will communicate life-changing lessons to you through it. Let us consider men whose eyes were opened to a great sight in the bible. These are men that saw 'ordinary' sights that transformed their lives into extraordinary expressions of God's power.

1. Moses and Nehemiah: The first pair of men I want to talk about in line with the great sight they saw are Moses and Nehemiah. Both men once lived in the palace and knew what royal splendour was like. Moses was Pharaoh's adopted grandson and an apparent heir to the throne, while Nehemiah was the king's official butler.

Both men had access to the highest powers of the world. In Moses' time, the Egyptian empire was the world power, while Media and Persia was the world power in the time of Nehemiah. Another thing they had in common was their antecedents. They were both Israelites; they were children of slaves in their respective lands.

But they understood the wills and the ways of God. Moses caught a vision for the enslaved Israelites and was so zealous about seeing them break free. This made God take him from Egypt to be trained first in the Wilderness before he later led the people of God from the land of slavery towards the land of freedom.

On the other hand, although his people were in slavery, Nehemiah didn't catch the vision to liberate his people. That was not his purpose; his purpose and vision were to rebuild the walls of Jerusalem, and the Lord rose up to help him do so. So one way to identify your purpose in God is by godly zeal.

Let us draw in closely on the incidents that transformed their lives. In Genesis 3, the bible tells us that while Moses kept the flock of his father-in-law, he saw a bush that was on fire but wasn't consumed. Such an unusual sight would have made some other people run away. But Moses did not run; instead, he was attracted to the sight and went close to it.

Every normal individual will follow logic, but because it is God calling you to a vision that will transform your life, you will not be able wave such an idea or a vision aside, it will be impressed upon your heart. And this is where the need for sensitivity arises; you must be sensitive to see and follow the sight the Lord has ordained to transform your life.

Nehemiah, on the other hand, was informed of the dilapidated state of the walls in Jerusalem by Hanani and it had a special effect on him. This is not because he's the king or someone important in the city of Jerusalem. He was just an ordinary citizen who had a deep compassion for the state of his nation. That deep compassion moved him to do something to better his country.

This is another method through which the Lord communicates vision to people. He impresses it upon their hearts and makes that impression trouble them till that impression causes such an individual to walk in the way God would have them walk. The questions you should ask yourself then are these: Where does your zeal consistently drive towards? What keeps you on your toe? What makes you lose comfort anytime it comes to mind?

That might as well be your purpose. So then, when this zeal rises in you, like Nehemiah, you might be ready, and God will give you all you need to fulfil your purpose in Him.

On the other hand, like Moses, you might have to go through a wilderness chapter that will cook you and make you ready to eat. Although zeal is an indicator of purpose, it is never enough. Zeal will never substitute for training. As I mentioned in the earlier chapter of this book, there is a need for training to work in the purpose God has for your life.

Your purpose does not have to be something big, and it doesn't have to be something gigantic; as far as it is from God, it is enough to span your lifetime. When compared to Moses, you might be tempted to think that Nehemiah's purpose and vision are more minor, but that's not true. Nehemiah's purpose is not more minor than Moses'. It is only different. Although most times they are complimentary; we all have unique purposes in life.

2. David and Solomon: Another set of biblical characters I would love to talk about in line with their purpose and vision is King David and Solomon's son. David inherited the throne of Israel not by birthright but by ordination from God. As a matter of fact, he had to fight many battles while he was king to maintain stability and balance in the land.

On the other hand, Solomon inherited the throne from and his father, and he didn't have to fight any battle throughout his reign. You must understand this: Solomon did not have to fight any battle doesn't mean that God is not with David. In the same vein, the fact that life seems easier for some Christians you know doesn't mean that God doesn't care about you. It can only mean that God is preparing you for different things. David was prepared in the Wilderness, but Solomon was built in the palace.

Furthermore, David had the zeal to build a temple for God, but God did not allow him. That was neither because God hated David nor because he offended God; it was simply because it was not his purpose. Instead, his purpose was to establish Jerusalem and the Davidic lineage of kings to represent godliness and holiness.

While Solomon, on the other hand, was allowed by God to build the temple. This is to show you that zeal is not an automatic pointer to purpose. You might be zealous about a thing, and it is not your purpose. God might have another way, asides from the one you think He will approve for you. That is why you must learn to hear Him.

The fact that Solomon built the temple doesn't mean that David is a failure. As a matter of fact, Solomon's construction of the temple proves that David succeeded both as a king and as a father. However, you must be careful not to fall into the error of measuring your purpose and vision by others around you. For example, every other person who is into evangelical ministry doesn't mean you will be an evangelist. Instead, God might be calling you to be an educator who will build lives for the glory of His name.

3. Peter and Paul: After the death, resurrection, and ascension of Christ, the church was moved by two significant figures. They were Peter and Paul. However, while Hod gave Peter and purpose amid the Jews, Paul was called to be an apostle among the gentiles.

At times, when things happen in our lives, we do not understand they are preparations in line with God's divine plan. When Christ was on earth, he put extra effort into making Peter and even mentioned that he had been given the keys of the kingdom of God. Simon was a name that means "a Reed," but the first time the Bible recorded that Jesus saw him, he named him Peter, "which means a rock."

When Jesus left the earth, Peter's ministry was amongst the news. He was sent to make them know the mystery of salvation through Christ and how to enter into it. He was sent to men who knew God's powers but did not fully understand His person. He was sent to bring back "the lost sheep of the house of Israel."

On the other hand, they encountered salvation miraculously when Jesus visited them on the way to Damascus. After that, he was built up in the knowledge of the truth by a few individuals like Ananias and Barnabas. So then Paul's purpose was between the gentiles. Those who had close to no knowledge about God.

The fact that Jews and gentiles had discrepancies between them as to how God can be accessed did not make Peter discredit Paul. On the contrary, Peter laboured silently amidst the news without ever talking down on Paul's purpose, and Paul laboured among the gentiles without trying to make himself more prominent than Peter.

Whatever God has called you to do, there is another person in the block. Such a person might be a co-labourer, or someone called into some other form of your ministry. You have not been sent to be seen; you have been sent that the glory of God might be revealed. You are not to try publicizing yourself so others can get important; however, you are to go with this mindset: "That I may decease and others through me increase."

Having drawn inferences from these lives regarding purpose and calling, it is needful to understand the secret of catching a Godly vision and maintaining it. Although it has been briefly mentioned in the earlier chapter of this book, it will be discussed in a more practical and applicable way here.

THE SECRET PLACE

The Bible says in Psalm 91:1 that, "He that dwells in the secret place of the most high will abide under the shadows of the almighty." In order words, if you make the secret place of God your go-to place, you will be covered by the almighty. Well, most people fit this Bible verse into the context of protection, and as accurate as that is, it is more than that.

The almighty's shadow is not limited only to his protection but also to his guidance and divine leading. This chapter has elaborately discussed how you need to walk in your God-ordained purpose and vision to thrive. I'll tell you this then; you will never walk in your God-given purpose if you have not learned to dwell in the secret place.

Dwelling in the secret place of God doesn't happen by wishes, neither does it happen by merely hoping. It takes deliberate action. It is easy for most people to visit the throne of grace and heal their needs and create a mole of prayer points. What is difficult is staying and remaining consistent in the secret place with God.

To dwell in the secret place of God is to deliberately dedicate your life to seeking Him and living for His glory. One of the things that inspired me most about the earthly life of Jesus is the level of dependency He had on God. Like, He was part of the Godhead, but He still made himself so dependent on God that He would ask His permission to do things and still rely on His name at all times.

One of the secrets of Jesus' life was revealed to us in Acts10:28. The Bible says, "How God anointed Jesus of Nazareth with the Holy Ghost and with power: who went about doing good and healing all that were oppressed of the devil; for **God was with him."** Although He carried the nature of God and was the express image of God's person, the secret of His success in life and ministry was not what He carried alone, but with whom He partnered.

God was always with Him. It doesn't matter whether he just lost a close friend and was mourning, or maybe he was invited to dinner with some tax collectors. He went everywhere with the presence of God. He already internalized God's presence and, by implication, His glory. So when Christ comes to a place, He comes in the name of the Lord.

Men who go far in God have learned the secret of tarrying in God's presence. They are not guests at the secret place, but they have made the secret place of the most high their dwelling place. The same was said of David and Joseph: "God was with him..." is God with you at all times, or He just fills you periodically and then leaves because you have learned to sustain His presence in the secret place?

The secret place is the place where men go to download instructions from God for a profitable living? Do you seek to know your purpose on this earth, be a man of the secret? Do you seek to receive a God-given vision that will guide and inform your life; storm the secret place, and dwell therein. Would you love your life to be an effulgence of God's? This also can only be found in a secret place with no other but God.

CHAPTER 3

CONCEIVING THE VISION

"Vision is the Source and hope of life. The greatest gift ever given to mankind is not the gift of sight, but the gift of vision. Sight is a function of the eyes; vision is a function of the heart. 'Eyes that look are common, but eyes that see are rare."

- Dr. Myles Munroe

THE BEAUTY AND POWER OF SIGHT

As earlier illustrated, God graciously created in us five sense organs, namely: the Eyes, the Ears, the Nose, the Tongue, and Skin. And these five sense organs contain receptors that relay information through the sensory neurons to the appropriate places within the nervous system.

Meanwhile, our Sight happens to be the most important of the five senses with the complex interaction between the brain and our eyes. This enables us to see and interact with the world around us and all its intricacies throughout our lives.

Before I go into detail about what a vision is, I'd like to walk you through the pathways of human sight. There are no better ways to explain the mind's creative power than to relate it to the physical world. Sight is a similar word to vision as I've briefly discussed previously.

Our senses are needed for accurate interaction with our surroundings. But among all the senses that God gave us, sight is the most important. The functions that come with visual ability can't be compared with anything in the world. Maybe this is the reason why God in his wisdom put our eyes at the top of our heads.

Human sight is a powerful tool. It gives clarity and confidence as we move from one place to another. For example, the reason why we can move without unnecessary carefulness is that we can see. The reason why we don't have to smell everything to know what's not sweet or fragrant is that we can see. The reason why we don't have to feel everything to know what will hurt us is that we can see. And the reason why we don't have to taste everything to know what is food is that we can see.

You may not understand the power of sight until you imagine how the blinds survive. Have you ever imagined how life would be if we couldn't see anything? Well, if you're able to walk around in your house this probably won't look like a big deal. Maybe closing your eyes till you get to your office will give you an idea of what it's like not to have eyesight. It's all darkness!

Moreover, in Genesis 1:2, the Bible stated three challenges on the then planet earth; it was **empty, in darkness, and shapeless**. These three problems can easily be perceived by sight, although one is directly connected to sight. If you would have to feel to determine if a large expanse of land is empty, it'd be almost impossible. But that'd even be unnecessary when you can sight emptiness, darkness, and shapelessness by easily looking at it. In another way, imagine going to a grocery store with your eyes closed, it'd be almost impossible to walk alone.

Now, if the physical eyes can bring so much meaning, precision, and beauty to our lives, how much more the eyes that can see farther? Simply put, the visual capacity that God gave us cannot be trivialized.

What about the freedom, confidence, and clarity that accompany the ability to see things, like knowing white from black? That's why, as humans, excellent vision is essential when it comes to ensuring a high quality of life. Two small eyeballs, but a wide range of sight! That's the beauty and power of sight.

THE EYES WITHIN

Now, did you know that as good as the physical human sight is, there's another eye we can see with? Yes, your mind is a greater sight. The mind cannot only see things, it can also create things. The greatest asset man has is the mind. The things the mind creates or conceives are called visions.

But sadly, not many with the two eyeballs working perfectly can conceive a vision that brings them success and breakthrough in life. That takes a deeper level of perception--not physical/normal eyesight. You see, not all eyes wide open have a vision for a lovely or desirable future. Normal eyes aren't capable of capturing a picture of the future.

You may want to ask, "What does it then mean to see?" If you have normal eyesight, you would probably think of sight as the ability to take a perfect picture of the world in front of you using your eyes. But that's not how vision works. Vision is generated from the inside out.

The world has witnessed a few physically blind people who caught a vision for their lives and rose to prominence.

Think about Daniel Kish, a man who was born with Retinoblastoma--an aggressive form of cancer that attacks the retinas, leading to vision loss. The young Daniel by 13 months old would have his eyes removed in a lifesaving operation. Despite the loss of sight, Daniel has his non-profit charity World

Access for the Blind organization. And by 2015, Kish's leadership and vision had already enabled the charity to introduce more than 500 students to echolocation. Notice! Without normal eyesight, he conceived and birthed a vision that has transformed many today. In the school of vision, therefore, physical sight isn't a major advantage.

I bet you, vision isn't a subject to take lightly—it defines whether or not you'll be great or remain small and irrelevant. Vision is so important in the circular sphere that CEOs and entrepreneurs often spend a great deal of time defining their visions, values, and goals. This is vital to a well-structured and highly competitive setup. The vision and goals formulate what they can do or not do. The scripture says, *"Where there is no prophetic vision the people cast off restraint..."* Proverbs 29:18.

WHAT THEN IS VISION?

According to Myles Munroe, "Purpose is when you know and understand what you were born to accomplish. Vision is when you see it in your mind and begin to imagine it." Yes, vision takes its mental ascent from an accurate understanding of purpose. When we talk of vision, it's the mental picture of what you want to achieve in life. It's like a road map that leads you down to your desired destination.

It's important to note that vision could be defined on short or long-term grounds. This picture must be vivid, clear, and intense in our minds to get the desired drive for stepping into the plane of success. Vision is a "turner" of dreams into a mentally achievable adventure. Make no mistake; vision isn't just a vague wish, dream, or hope for a better life. For a Christian, vision is sourced from God. It takes a renewed mind to access God's bank of good counsel.

When you have a vision, it brings energies and beauties of the future to your present—making you willing to sacrifice and let go of anything for the moment. Two brave figures in the scriptures bring me great inspiration—Jesus and Paul. One thing that characterized their lives was the ability to sustain a focus and vision no challenge could hamper. The Bible says something interesting about Jesus in the book of Hebrews 12:2, *"Looking unto Jesus, the author, and finisher of our faith, who for the joy that was set before Him endured the cross, despising the shame, and has sat down at the right hand of the throne of God."*

Following the joy that was set or placed before Jesus--as the end of His ministry on earth, paying the price to get there wasn't a big deal. A clear vision for your life colors the sufferings of the moment and makes it a beautiful part of your success story. Yes, that's what vision does. It has the power to transfuse supernatural strength into the vision carrier.

Conceiving a vision is the beginning and the most potent foundation to lay in the school of success. Without it, all that is done is a mere guess-walk. And guess-walk never produces excellent results. Any success you have in life must begin with a clear vision--the ability to see what others cannot see and walk the paths others dread to walk. Therefore doing what others thought impossible!

YOUR VISUAL CAPACITIES

It's important to note that your sight is different from your vision. Generally, sight entails the physical - a sensory experience in which light reflects off of objects and shapes, and the eyes then focus on the light. Signals are sent from the brain to be converted into images. Vision is how the mind, an aspect of the brain, interprets these images. Vision is metaphysical. Sight allows a person to witness an event, but vision helps the person understand the significance of that event and draw interpretations. The two are harmonious and are very important in our everyday lives.

> **The significance of vision in your success.**

Your progress in anything is largely determined by what you can see. Consider the light that is attached to your car. It's nearly impossible to drive at night without it. And, of course, because eyesight is an active sensor, it relies on sunlight to see, we can drive during the day. This is a representation of how we live. Our journey is guided and clarified my vision. One fundamental truth about success is that it is never an accident.

The majority of the accidents you've witnessed before are due to miscalculation, mechanical fault, or any other unprecedented reasons. But I'm not sure if anyone will have an accident planned except in movies. Any form of navigation requires sight or sensing and reasoning, whether or not automated. You simply can't be successful without first having a clear mental picture of what you want to achieve.

You wonder why so many people are running from one place to another, hoping to come across an oasis someday. Living in this manner is akin to driving at night without a headlight and assuming that the road is smooth, straight, and free. What a dreadful assumption! It will not only get you into trouble, but the crash will be excruciating. Even though seeing life isn't just a physical thing but movement and progress are solely guided by the ability to see what's along the way. Indeed, we can't see the future, even if it's only a split second away, but the mind is powerful and creative enough to create mental pictures and imaginations that help you navigate life. Visions provide you with a creative imagination for many years ahead.

The account of Genesis reveals the different kinds of people who had lived many years before us. Although many names are mentioned, only a few contribute to the stories. What a challenge! The commonest storyline in the very beginnings of Genesis is '... And some lived years, and begat so many sons, and died.' But there were men whose lives transcended history, such are the ones we read about today, not the ones whose cycle was predictable.

One of them being Abraham. Abraham was a man like us, in fact probably older than us at the time when God called him. One day God summoned him to take a look at the sky, and when he lifted his eyes, he saw stars so many that he couldn't take his eyes off. There were too many to count. He had no idea what that meant until God revealed to him that his seeds were similar to what he had just seen.

At some point, he told him to look far. Visions, as I've said earlier, function by sight. Your eyes are very important in conceiving your visions. Our eyes and minds can work together to fully capture God's mind for us, only if we open our hearts. It is impossible to live a purposeful life without a vision because vision is the light that guides us on our journey of destiny. Your vision will propel you until you reach the pinnacle in God. But how can you live if you're not sure why you're alive?

The power of vision isn't so much in its perfection and full grasp on what the future holds. Sometimes, it comes in bits. Yes, Joseph had a vision to run with, but a chunk of that vision wasn't revealed until much later in the land of slavery. Truth is, so much power is embedded in the conception of vision—it gives meaning to life and ignites the spirit of man. Power and confidence is sponsored by a clear conception of a vision for life.

Vision and sight aren't only so important because they actively allow us to connect with our environment, help maintain aptness and enable us to stay away from danger.

There's a popular saying that the eyes are the windows of the soul. This expression is one we use more often than not when we're describing the immense connection we feel when we look into another person's eyes. Similarly, the eyes can see deeper things when strongly connected to the soul. Is it okay if I tell you that your eyes aren't only meant to see things but to see deep? Meanwhile, your mind isn't also only meant for thinking but for thinking deeply.

THE BEAUTY OF YOUR LIFE

This world has seen billions of individuals pass through it. How many of them can we say lived their lives to the fullest and purposely? And when I speak of a fulfilled life, I mean a life that is driven and inspired by the kingdom perspective, intending to bring glory to God and blessings to humanity.

I'm also not referring to celebrities, but rather to purpose-driven men. One of the many reasons why people fail is that they are never satisfied with their uniqueness. Some eventually fail to realize their uniqueness. They become consumed by others' success and achievements. Their lives make no sense to them. While these individuals are attempting to copy others or are being dissatisfied with themselves, a few individuals eventually get it right and leave their names on the precious stones of time.

When you think about men in our modern age, you'll see several vision-driven individuals who had a vision for life and ran with it? Many Believers, like Biblical heroes, pressed beyond their immediate circumstances and limitations. Think about Ben Carson, the first black neurosurgeon.

Most people didn't believe Ben Carson would achieve much with his life when he was a kid. He was impoverished, received low grades, and got into a lot of trouble. But Ben was fortunate in one way: he had a mother who believed in him and pushed him to strive harder and be more determined. Ben was able to overcome his rough early years because of her encouragement and support. He decided to pursue the insurmountable, and he went on to become one of the top pediatric neurosurgeons in the world!

What about women like Kathryn Kuhlman? She was only fourteen years old when she had her first spiritual encounter. She pursued her passion and later became an itinerant preacher in Idaho. Kathryn Kuhlman was a faith healer, orator, and evangelist. She was a well-known preacher who was well-known for her healing gifts.

All great people have one thing in common—they had a unique vision and ran with it. They're special today, not because they bear different names but because of the conceptualization and actualization of their vision. In other words, where vision is missing, nothing striking can be done. We can tell their stories today because they had a goal for which they lived their lives.

Truth is, we only remember those who leave their imprints on our hearts not those who merely left an impression. Their vision is the beauty of their life. The sweet memories of them we have are the ones that many might have doubted them for when they didn't look like it.

CONCEIVE IT, BELIEVE IT

> *"Whatever your mind can conceive and believe, it can achieve"*
>
> - Napoleon Hill's

The story of Caleb and Joshua constantly challenges me. In the book of Numbers 13, Moses sends twelve spies to look out the Promised Land and bring report of the state of the land. Surprisingly, only two—Caleb and Joshua—out of twelve came with a good report. Imagine writing an open test with scholars and 80% of your class choose A, while 20%, including you, choose B. In the test, your answer will determine whether or not you'll be promoted to the next class. With the majority going for the first option, if you're not confident of your answer, I bet you may doubt it and choose wrongly. Is it possible that 80% of the class miss the answer or are you the one missing it?

Caleb and Joshua have a lot to teach us today about what we conceive and believe. All right, let's begin with the mentality. Vision requires faith from the beginning to the end.

After surveying the land of Canaan, the twelve spies reported to Moses and the Israelites with their findings. The crowd was giddy with excitement. God Himself had guided them up from Egypt, and the decisive moment had arrived. Moses had sent out the spies forty days previously, with instructions to gather as much information as possible before the Israelites entered the country to claim it as their own. "Be of good courage," he said as he left. "And bring some of the land's produce."

And here they were, carrying a cluster of grapes so huge that it had to be carried by two men! "We traveled to the land you sent us to. It flows with milk and honey, and this is the product of its labor." People came in a frenzy to see for themselves. Everyone wanted a piece of the fruit!

Consider all the things God had shown the people of Israel, yet it was hard for almost all of them but Caleb and Joshua to believe that the land was for them.

God can speak to us anytime even in the hard times. But sometimes, we often get carried away that we don't focus on His words for our lives. We hardly conceive good things for ourselves when we have bad feelings. Even though we change, the God in the good times is still God in the bad times. Why do you doubt your vision? The truth is, if you don't believe in your vision because there are no physical proofs for their fulfillment you can't birth them. We doubt God's predestined plan for our lives just because we don't look like it.

You cannot have the appropriate vision unless you have the right attitude. Have you ever sought advice from many persons to find out that each person's advice opposed another's? This is because everyone thinks differently, and our mindset influences our thoughts.

God cannot help those who refuse to believe in his purpose for their lives. He has much too much regard for the free will He has bestowed on us. In reality, it is impossible to satisfy God without faith. On the other hand, He lavishes gifts on those who seek Him with zeal.

REFIXING YOUR EAGLE-SIGHT

Eagles are a beautiful breed in the class of birds. They have majestic frames and incredible hunting abilities. One fascinating fact about the eagles is that they have the reputation of having one of the best vision on the planet. According to PBS—Public Broadcasting Service—the earth has 59 different species of eagles. Every species with a different degree of visual acuity is far superior to that of most other animals—humans included. Several eagle species can spot rabbits—a favorite prey—as far as 2 miles away and can easily detect the movements of field mice while flying as high as 650 feet above the ground.

Amazingly, eagles don't just step out of their nest on a goose chase. You see, just like an Eagle, vision and understanding must be the driving factor to every of your flight and action. Personal success begins with setting a flawless vision. Here is a piece of advice: before you step out daily, be intentional about what you intend to do or accomplish that day. That's a critical success factor. Eagles have excellent vision and concentration. To catch their prey, they focus on it with laser-like intensity and set out to get it. What listen can we draw from here? Do the same with your goals. Focus on one thing to accomplish at a time. Give it your effort, time, and energy. Focus and "set out to achieve it".

Eagles can see far—you must too! Successful people have the power of focus, foresight, clarity of vision just like the Eagle can see objects as far as 5 kilometers away.

In the world today, a lot of things can be tagged as a distraction. Nonetheless, to be successful in today's world it's imperative to remain dogged and tenacious so be able to achieve your goal. You need to have a vision and a focus to be successful.

KEEP THE RIGHT LENSES

For an optimum vision of where you're going in life, choosing and keeping the right lenses is essential. According to Carl Zeiss, while many vision problems could limit visual perception, an optimally fitted pair of glasses with the right lenses can help see once more. How true this is when we talk about sustainable visionary drive.

While many problems becloud human's sense of vision today, the Christian is provided with chunks of divine lenses in God's word for suitable visionary living. King David so vividly captured this when he said "thy word is a lamp to my feet and a light that brightens my path."

You don't just cook up a fantastic design and tag its vision. It must be God-given for it to have God's results. To get and keep the right lenses for peeping into the future with such clarity and sense of duty, it must begin from accessing God's mind for what He fashioned you to be in life through His Word. I mean, a Christian x conceives a true vision not just by self-discovery but God's discovery.

When you're able to peep into your identity in God, you wouldn't walk down life with a blurry vision of your destination and what you want in life. God's word is the most accurate lenses a believer must and should take on to access a vision that transcends time and the mundane. Habakkuk 2:2 *"And the Lord answered me: "Write the vision; make it plain on tablets, so he may run who reads it."* Keep your lenses on for optimum perception!

CHAPTER 4

GET RID OF SUCCESS CLUTTERS

"Clutter is nothing more than a postponed decision."

- Barbara Hemphill

Have you discovered that not everyone you show unrestrained affection always expresses it back? What about those who constantly hurt you yet you keep close to your heart--you couldn't just let them go! Are there not many people you feel you should let go, but haven't decided when to let them go? When you found out that you've got a habit that impedes success, why haven't you dealt it a decisive blow? That skill and professional course you felt would boost your success tag, what's keeping you mute and merely wishful getting it?

Postponed decisions breed clusters in your life and render you ineffective and impotent for your business and adventure through life. Successful people know how to exterminate every deadly pest in the field of success before casting their precious seed of time and investment. Before they get committed to anyone and any course, they watch and measure what level of impact it would breed on their success story. Knowing that not many people can travel the lonely road of success makes you choose who to commit your time and energy to. The school of fish swims together, and the colony of bats flocks together.

Success is company-fussy! You don't want to be an Eagle moving with bats with their head to the ground of pity and laziness! You want to maintain a depth of intensity and a calculated risk-taking drive. You know, on your success trip, many tend to be upset when you refuse to drop off your principles to accommodate their excesses or join their misery. You've got to get unapologetic to pull the needed strength for a successful life.

HOW VALUABLE IS YOUR VISION?

Are valuables kept casually where all could see and touch them? Truth is, Value always excites uniqueness and some sort of pride. That is to say that it's how valuable your vision is to you that defines the sort of persons you allow into your vaulted success space.

Have you ever visited the bank and been granted access to the bank vault? That may never happen in your lifetime. A bank vault is a protected space where money, valuables, records, and documents are stored. The major aim of vaults is to protect the bank's valuables from theft, fire, unauthorized use, natural disasters, or other threats.

Not everybody will add to your vision or success story. Hence, your commitment level to people must be defined by how relevant they are to the fulfillment of your purpose and vision. You must deliberately erect a success vault around your vision; bringing about limited access. You must decisively raise a stern hedge against prying distractions. You see, clutters here are all the things/people who may hinder your effectiveness in the pursuit of the fulfillment of your vision. They are like piggish rodents against your vision--erect healthy personal and relationship boundaries that safeguard your vision.

Let's get more personal here. After you conceive a vision, know your goals, and priorities in life, then everything that is out of place and not in keeping with your vision is cluttering you. You must then declutter all. So, when you declutter having identified what clutters are around your vision, everything becomes so much easier.

You don't spend your time with people with a myopic perception of life or folks that bring you down—constantly talking less of your vision. Never become a victim of Joseph-naivety. He was seeking succor and motivation from anger-infested sources. He told His vision to his brothers and it spurred bitterness and wrath. Get this clear! Not everyone close to you will get fascinated by your vision. Living a life that protects and guard vision against conception to fruition has become increasingly difficult in the 21st-century internet craze world.

Even though you may prioritize having a social life with family and friends, clearly spell out your space and bar anyone causing you more hassle than help—they are clutters. Another clutter to get rid of is the misunderstanding of doing a thing because you've always done it. You need time alone, like Jesus, to pray and do some strategic thinking to know your valiant 12 out of the 70 willing men drawn to you. Jesus never lived for the crowd. He was only committed to, spent more time with, and communicated deep matters about His vision with the disciples in His inner circle.

Truth is, you're only as good as the company you keep. You probably have heard the saying "birds of a feather flock together." That simply implies that similar people gravitate to each other. When you surround yourself with smart people, you'll expand your proficiency and competence; you'll have a bolster community that will nudge you towards becoming a better version of yourself. Just like a foam soaks in water in an ocean, you'll always soak up the interests, goals, and expertise of those in your 'Ships'—friendship, relationship, or partnership.

Success breeds more success. *"As iron sharpens iron, so one person sharpens another."* Proverbs 27:17.

Many times, having an unnecessary coalition with people brings a lot to take up your headspace. Meanwhile, scattered and disorganized plans leave your mind cluttered with your unprecedented or processed thoughts. Wouldn't it be better to get your thoughts, inspirations, ideas, and plans down in a planner/diary and free up the space in your mind again? You will feel so much better having them in the 'right' place!

DECLUTTERING TO FLY HIGH

Remember we talked about the Eagle in the previous chapter? For Eagles to fly high, all clutter that hinders freedom of flight is taken out. More so, Eagles fly alone and with their kind. The vision-flight rule is: **"Only associate with people who travel at your pace or even faster."** At your pace to make you steady and focused, and faster to motivate and challenge you to grow and do more.

Because not everyone will share your vision or dream, locating and discerning people who think like you so that you can both dream and grow together becomes vital. Don't waste your time with naysayers and negative people. And don't share your dreams with just anybody. You've got a dream? Protect and guard it!

Even though Eagles are in the class of birds, they don't fly with other species of birds--they live and fly on a frequency no ordinary bird can dare to fly. Valley or low thinking isn't the reality of the Eagle-company at all. Negative thinking is a clutter you must be decluttered from. Eagles ride on the fears of the wind that sends many birds into hiding. Cowards don't make an impact. They only leave impressions in people's minds and that doesn't last long.

You see, you've got to get your identity clear and leverage your hidden potentials to fly high altitude. Lack of identity is one of the enemies of success. Be clear about your identity and what you stand for. You need to know and understand yourself and be mindful of the kind of company you keep. The Bible reveals that *"He who works with the wise shall be wise and a companion of fools shall be destroyed."* Show me your friends and companies and I will predict your future.

Another fascinating fact I found out about Eagles is that they test the level of commitment before engagement. Before entering into a commitment, the female eagle tests her male suitors to establish his level of commitment. Wow! When last did you test the level of people's commitment to your vision before you partner with them? I call partnership with the commitment test "blind-trust." When trust isn't a result of tests and validation, you throw your life into a boat destined for sinking.

We have several characters in scriptures who almost ran into problems because they didn't deal with clutters on their path to success. They tried many times to take off with their wings tied to a pole of unnecessary relationship. Think about Joseph. "Joseph had a dream, and when he told it to his brothers, they hated him all the more." (Genesis 37:5) He never knew that his brothers were his success clutters. He trusted them with his vision and he almost got killed. Joseph was too childish to conceive a vision. So, he let the cat out of the box before it was time.

It was his father that shut him down--teaching us that not everyone is worthy of knowing your vision at conception. They'll get to know when it starts speaking. "For the vision is yet for an appointed time, but at the end, it shall speak, and not lie: though it tarry, wait for it; because it will surely come, it will not tarry." Habakkuk 2:3. No vision speaks at the beginning. It's rather despised or belittled by ignorant men. The Bible talks about the days of little beginnings "Do not despise these small beginnings, for the Lord rejoices to see the work begin, to see the plumb line in Zerubbabel's hand." (Zachariah 4:10).

Guess why Jonathan died at the battle of Mount Gilboa along with his father and brothers? (1 Samuel 31). Inability to declutter! It's so pathetic that Jonathan got killed in battle simply because he was in the wrong company. Good intention isn't a guarantee for the fulfillment of the vision. You must be mindful of the people you tell your vision to—you don't need multitude in your success birthing room—just your success midwife is enough!

Think about a woman in the birthing room, does she need a crowd of people in the room? No! You just need a professional, skillful, and passionate midwife—all those other folks who are passionless and are like scaffolds don't need to get into your birthing space. Many times, we want so badly to bring everyone with us to success. But in fact, not everyone is ready for success nor can they handle the commitments that characterize its realization. So, it's about being careful about who you take along on your path to success. Not everyone is interested in your success. You've got to give limited access to your life!

VANGUARD YOUR INNER CIRCUIT

"Afterward Jesus went up on a mountain and called out the ones he wanted to go with him. And they came to him."
- Mark 3:13

Think about the scripture above. Jesus called out only those he wanted to go with Him on His adventure. Jesus knew perfectly that not many people will be interested in His vision neither will they be able to handle the sacrifices that beautify success. And indeed, when Jesus began to step into the depths of His vision, even Judas betrayed Him. Stones of hate and criticism thrown at you from outsiders may never disrupt your vision. But the ones generated from your inner caucus can deal you a deadly blow.

Meanwhile, the people who encircle you speak to your values, beliefs, and goals. In other words, you can be guilty by association. It's very important to choose the right group of friends and confidants to be with through your stage of conception and realization of your vision. Jim Rohn, an American entrepreneur and author, once said "You are the average of the five people you spend the most time with." Those in your inner circle are the most trusted people in your life.

Finally, these people may include your family members, friends, neighbors, and professional colleagues. They impact your attitudes and behaviors. Colin Powell said, "A mirror reflects a man's face, but what he is really like is shown by the kind of friends he chooses." Wow! I so much love this quote. You see, you'll eventually think like they do and behave as they behave. When it comes to relationships, we are greatly influenced. Your relationships impact how you think, your self-esteem, and your decisions.

Vision is a natural transit between the present and the future. It raises new questions, paradigm shifts, and even births new relationships. It demands how you spend your time. Regardless of age or phase of life, vision may catalyze to force your behaviors to line with the person you want to become.

Friendships, too, maybe reviewed and made more valuable by classifying them appropriately to meet their value. Allow me to explain.

UNDERSTANDING DESTINY RELATIONSHIPS

Friendships can be classified into variety of ways. Many people have shared a friend categorization that I found amusing but extremely useful in context. Some stated that there are "three-minute friends," "three-hour friends," and "three-day friends." We can regard each friendship group as vital to a person's vision, but only when properly classified.

For example, a 3-minute acquaintance is a coworker who engages in conversation about last week's football match but has no obligation to enquire about anything more serious in your private affairs. And that may be a good thing! But, be assured, you would not like to spend a weekend camping alone with a three-minute friend. That would not only be unpleasant, but it may also be harmful in terms of vision-driven relationships.

Now let's dive deep into relationships. There are five classes of relationships you'd come across especially if you're particular about having friends that are godly and driven by vision. They're called the 5 C's Relationships.

➢ The Confidants

"One who has unreliable friends soon comes to ruin, but there is a friend who sticks closer than a brother." Proverbs 18:24

Confidants are those who surround you because they are interested in you. They believe in you as an individual and will stand by your side regardless of your failure. Confidants are always all in for you, and the only reason they might leave you is if they can't get enough of you or your friendship. They come into your space fully committed to you and your vision. You'll never get a down moment with them—they constantly keep you on your toes and encouraged.

They are, nonetheless, clever enough to point out when you are mistaken. The Confidants are with you for the foreseeable future. They come into your life and stay with you until the end of your life. They don't come to you to assist with a specific mission and then leave. They come into your life because they believe in you.

Confidants are the individuals in your life who actually support you! They come just for, nothing more! Confidants adore you without reservation. They're interested in you. Whether you are right or wrong, up or down. They are committed to you for the long term. If you make a mess, they will join you in your messiness. You may open up to them and discuss everything without fear of being criticized. You can trust them so much that you can be yourself with them just as much as you do when you're alone. You will never be all that you can be in life until you accept this challenge.

You will never realize your full potential in life unless you discover your Confidant. Although they may not always concur with you, they will always support and want to inspire you to become the greatest version of yourself in all aspects of your life.

➢ The Constituents

Constituents are people that surround you because they support your cause. They are folks who are following the same goal as you are, heading to the same location as you are, and hence walking the same road as you are. They are just with you since you are all heading in the same direction. In other words, Constituents are the people that come into your life by the privilege of your direction. They are with you because of where you are going which is also where they are heading, and if by any chance they find someone or something else that guarantees them a faster journey than you, they will abandon you for that specific individual or thing. They are those that support what you stand for! Constituents are critical to moving your concept forward. And, if you believe in what they believe in, they will happily walk with you, work with you, and solve problems with you. They will not, however, be with you indefinitely. Constituents will depart from you when someone or something better works in their favor, regardless of the period in your life. As a result, do not base your life plans on them.

➢ The Commanders

Commanders, on the other hand, are those that surround you because you have a commodity that can get them where they need to go. They are around you not because you're heading where they're heading, but rather because you have a commodity or expertise that they believe will be useful in assisting them in reaching their objective. Commanders, like Constituents, quit you whenever they encounter someone or something that offers to get them to their target destination faster than you.

They may also leave you if they no longer require your services or have discovered a higher-quality supply somewhere else. A critical point to note about people who are commanders in your life is that they only come into your life when they need your expertise, skills, or something they feel you're the only one who can give it to them. This kind of people are deadly to the birthing of your vision. You don't want to sell your vision to them. Don't you think so?

The point is, you don't make enemies out of people who are commanders in your life. People who want to just be in charge of your space and influence every of your decision to satisfy them must be dreaded and kept away from your birthing room, I must say. You should create necessary boundaries that keep such deadly folks out of your success space for maximum impact and deployment of our energies for the actualization of our vision.

I believe it's your responsibility to determine whether or not you allow commanders access into your life. As much as you want to be nice to people, care for them, and make them feel happy, be sensitive not to throw your vision into a vast ocean of distrust. (Matthew 5: 41-46; 1Peter 2:18).

➢ The Comrades

Finally, comrades are people who surround you because they oppose what you oppose. They are people that surround you because you are both fighting the same adversary. They are just with you to witness the defeat of the stronger foe. They are like scaffold that is set in position to erect a structure. The scaffold is disassembled once the construction is completed. When the adversary is defeated, the companions depart. They will join you in your struggle against a common foe.

These are not for what you stand for, but rather against it. They are crucial for keeping an eye on your back and safeguarding you from invisible dangers. But don't be misled by their affiliation; they will only stay with you till triumph is achieved. Comrades will stay with you until the adversary is defeated, so be willing to let them all go in peace whenever the time arrives. These people are similar to scaffolding. They are extremely near to you and enter your life to accomplish a reason; after that function is fulfilled, the scaffolding is removed. Don't get too worked up over it. The building remains after the scaffolding is removed.

> The Clutters

Vision Clutters aren't necessarily things. Some people are pungent to our vision. They literally don't have anything to contribute, they can only be burdensome. This set of people come to destroy your vision. They will utterly discourage you until you have nothing to live for. You can easily know them because you don't have common values and standards.

Being aware of the classes of destiny relationships in your life can help you relate with people accordingly and put them in their place. It is great Wisdom to be able to categorize your friends or the individuals surrounding you into Confidants, Comrades, Commanders and Constituents, to love them all as God has told us in Matthew 22:39, and to conduct them according to their classifications.

The only significant danger with Constituents and Comrades is misclassification. When you view any of them to be "**Confidants**," you may be on the verge of heartbreak when they leave you for another, greater cause. This is one of the reasons why many individuals refuse to let strangers in. It might be difficult to distinguish between the Constituent and the Comrade and the Confidant since they appear so similar.

Confidants are unique! They are so profoundly unique that they embrace you with a desire of brilliance whatsoever, whether you reveal a weakness or a strength! You'll just have a couple of them, which is OK. You are an outlier if you only have two or three of them throughout your lifetime. And, since there is only so much time and energy available to genuinely return this degree of interpersonal privilege, you cannot successfully be committed to even more than a few Confidants.

➢ How to Spot the Right Friends

Some characteristics can help you identify the friends who are critical to your success. They are attentive listeners who allow you to express yourself freely. They allow you time to extricate your soul without delivering random thoughts or deviating from the issue. They ask inquiries instead of offering recommendations. They advise you on how to improve your chances of success. Some friends would even provide you instances or anecdotes to make such suggestions without pushing on you.

When you need someone, a good friend will not make you wait. If they are unable to assist you for whatever reason; they will contact you as soon as possible. Genuine friends have no doubts about you or your goals. They strive to assist in every way they can. They may be excellent critics, but their intentions are always noble. Recognizing your genuine friends will make life easier and allow you to obtain the honest feedback you need to achieve.

HOW CAN YOU GET CLOSER TO YOUR MOTIVATORS?

Consider spending significant time with the people in your circle of friends and family who are significant. Finding the time for those who genuinely care is a method of expressing thanks.

Schedule time for people who will support and challenge like you would any other assignment. On weekends, pay a visit to your parents or other close relatives. At least three to four times every week, have lunch or supper with your family. Finding shared interests with them will also help you become closer to them.

Success is determined by the people you surround yourself with. Encouragement and empathy from friends or family members can undoubtedly help you achieve more in life. They will pay heed to you, reassure you, and give answers to your concerns.

DECLUTTER!

7 POWER REFLECTION QUESTIONS/PROMPTINGS TO HELP YOU DECLUTTER

1. Can you list out all the people around you who have never made significant input into your life but take a chunk of your time and declutter them immediately?

2. What are the things that exhaust your time and energy but never impact your vision and drive? Write them down and write them off your priority list!

3. Who are your midwives? Think and reflect deeply about this and get more committed to them.

4. What lessons can you learn from the life of Jesus about how He structured His relationship system and commitment to people around Him? List some down AND imbibe them.

5. What inner resolution do you need to make to sustain a growing and positive relationship with your inner circuits?

6. List out your core values, trademarks, and the uniqueness you'll never alter to accommodate naysayers' suggestions and discouraging words.

7. Make a list of things you'll never give a yes to because of your vision and pursuit. Can you make a decision not to allow anyone talk you out of the demands of the fulfillment of your vision? It's your time to take the Eagle-flight! SOAR!!

CHAPTER 5

BIRTHING YOUR VISION

"Son of man, what is this proverb that ye have in the land of Israel, saying, the days are prolonged, and every vision faileth? Tell them therefore, Thus saith the Lord Jehovah: I will make this proverb to cease, and they shall no more use it as a proverb in Israel; but say unto them, The days are at hand and the fulfillment of every vision.."

- Ezekiel 12:22-23 (ASV)

In the world today, childbirth is most fraught with anxiety and fear for mothers to be. Even though conception for married couples is often a well-anticipated experience, childbirth is like a high mountain many pray to climb without losing strength. According to a 2015 investigation carried out by USA Today, "Approximately 800 women in the USA die each year during pregnancy and within 42 days after delivery." What staggering statistics this is!

Friends, when you think of the number of Christians who never see the fruition of their vision, you'll be more alarmed. Yes, vision is a dire requisite for success, life, and destiny. However, it's not enough to conceive a vision, it's vital to have the vision fulfilled. Think about the number of believers who grow into their grey years with unfulfilled desires and visions. Why do we constantly fall into the class of princes Solomon talked about in Ecclesiastes 10:7? He said, "I have seen slaves on horseback while noblemen go on foot like slaves." (GNB)

When a man with such identity as a nobleman lacks the intelligence to come into the place of understanding, he walks as a mere man even though full of kingly promises. This is because if a vision must be fulfilled, it must be powered by divine principles unto the fulfillment. Wishful thinking and a good intention aren't strong grounds for breeding and fulfillment of a divine vision. Meanwhile, many will have no struggles conceiving a vision—knowing the city—knowing how to get there is the great stumbling block. It was the wise-man Solomon that described the labor of a man that conceived a vision of the desired land but was devoid of the knowledge of how to get there. He puts it this way: "The labor of fools wearieth every one of them; for he knoweth not how to go to the city." (Ecclesiastes 10:15) Notice!

Knowing the city (which is synonymous with conceiving a vision) isn't the problem here; it's the "how" problem.

Hence, in this last chapter, I will show you biblical steps woven into principles for the fulfillment of your divine vision and mandate. This will surely be a life-changing closure—a definite end that redefines the myopic perception of life and vision. Let's get started right away!

DOES GOD CARE?

To start with, I have some critical questions to settle here—Does God wants the believer to be successful? Is God committed to granting you success in the actualization of your vision? Let's take a look at a few scriptures to glean some wisdom.

First, Romans. 8:37 makes it clear that the believer isn't just struggling to become a victor or successful, God had already granted the believer success in Christ. "He made you more than conquerors through Christ He always leads you in triumph in Christ." Let that truth sink in, friend—that's a good place to start your journey into actualization. From start, you must know that you won already. Glory to God!

I love what Paul, by the Spirit of God, unveiled in 2 Corinthians 2:14. It captured the resources kept in God for the fulfillment of anything that pertains to life and godliness for the believer. "He has given you everything you need for life and godliness." Because God knows all you need for the fulfillment of your divine vision, He packaged it in Christ for you in bits of wisdom and nuggets of truth—access them!

Apostle Peter added, "He (God) has blessed you with every spiritual blessing in heavenly places in Christ Jesus" 2 Pet. 1:3. Wow! Think about that—the bible said ALL. You may wonder how this relates to the fulfillment of your vision. Coast on, let me explain. How could you fulfill a divine assignment and mandate without spiritual resources made available? What God gifts men as blessings isn't defined by earthly standards—it's spiritual blessings. But then, when you come into this economy of God's blessing, to fulfill your purpose will look like a walk in the park—no stress at all!

Ephesians 1:3 revealed God's commitment more—"The Holy Spirit helps you in your weakness." Nobody fails that's helped by God. Even in your weak moments in the pursuit of your vision, God still says, "I am committed!" Why? Romans. 8:26 answers the question. "For His strength is perfected in your weakness." Friend, do these verses sound like God wants you to fail? Never! God cares and you must first leverage that divine advantage in the birthing of your vision.

BIBLICAL PRINCIPLES TO SUCCESSFUL VISION

What are principles and why are they so important? Cambridge Dictionary has a profound definition of this concept. A Principle is "a basic idea or rule that explains or controls how something happens or works." Principles have no respect for age, class, or spirituality. When the principles that govern success are neglected or taken lightly, trying to make a visual work would be like trying so hard to empty an ocean with a cup.

The truths that govern success must be fully obeyed and subscribed to for having lasting and desired results. Principles help you maintain a concentrated focus in the fulfillment of your vision. Success can be repeated and maintained when goodly principles are imbibed. Imagine a farmer who skipped the time of planting, will he ever experience the joy of reaping a harvest? No! And why? He broke the law of sowing before reaping.

Now, let's see the principles that ease the births of visions. We will only see 4 principles here, although there are more scattered through the pages of scriptures.

1. Counting the cost

"For which of you, desiring to build a tower, doth not first sit down and count the cost, whether he have wherewith to complete it? Lest haply, when he hath laid a foundation and is not able to finish, all that behold begin to mock him, saying, this man began to build, and was not able to finish." (Luke 14:28-30). Think about what Jesus said here. Birthing your vision isn't going to be possible if you haven't subscribed to a deep understanding of what it will cost you to achieve success.

You've got the mental picture of where you want to be. Now, get yourself a good strategic notepad to outline all you see as needed resources for building this towering vision. Don't start what you wouldn't be able to finish. To start on the journey of birthing your vision and get stuck in the middle of the way will attract serious mockery. Get into your war-room and draw your battle plan under God. Do you have what it takes to start up that firm or corporation? If not, give it a pause until you're sure you've set for it!

2. Grace and Labor

"If the Lord does not build a house, then those who build it work in vain. If the Lord does not guard a city, then the watchman stands guard in vain. It is vain for you to rise early, come home late, and work so hard for your food. Yes, he can provide for those whom he loves even when they sleep." Psalm 127:1-2 (NET).

When is the labor of men in vain? When labor goes in without God's impute of grace and blessings. You can do nothing if you're disconnected from the source of all grace.

God gives grace to men that they may labor into their prophesied places. But it's pathetic that many believers talk so much about grace and neglect the place of work/labor. Even though God gave Apostle Paul grace, he equated that grace to more labor. If grace multiplies over life, it's so that you can expand your capacity to labor. He said, "But by the grace of God I am what I am: and his grace which was bestowed upon me was not found vain; but I labored more abundantly than they all: yet not I, but the grace of God which was with me." (1 Corinthians 15:10)

No vision gets fulfilled without grace coupled with labor. "The horse is prepared for the day of battle, but the victory belongs to God." (Proverbs 21:31) Because the Lord gives victory doesn't mean men shouldn't prepare the horse for the day of battle. God's giving of strength and grace must make a man do the needful. It isn't God that prepares the horse—you do! You must identify everything needed for the realization of your vision and give yourself to it. If you need to learn new skills, invest in needed books/materials, or take up professional courses—please do. Prepare your horse for the day of battle!

3. Diligence; a key principle

"Seest thou a man diligent in his business? He shall stand before kings; He shall not stand before mean men." Proverbs 22:29. Diligence is the careful and persistent work or effort you give to a course to see it birth the desired result. Many believers have a fleeting robotic attitude that keeps them ever small and unproductive. The bible says only a man who understands diligence in his business will step into greatness.

God is not in a party with lazy folks! "Lazy people always want things but never get them. Those who work hard get plenty."- Proverbs 13:4 (ERV). The Good News Bible puts it this way; "No matter how much a lazy person may want something, he will never get it. A hard worker will get everything he wants." Without this principle woven into your character, the pursuit of vision will never bring full color. God told Adam, "keep your Garden and tend it." No room for lazy folk in the land flowing with milk and honey.

4. Give and make more rooms

If there's a topic many Christian do not like to hear anymore—here's one! Giving is the key that unlocks God's warehouse of blessing to any man. We never give to help God but to cause an explosion of God's blessings to be poured out on us! Giving means making rooms for more divine supplies. Jesus said, "Give to others, and God will give to you. Indeed, you will receive a full measure, a generous helping, poured into your hands—all that you can hold. The measure you use for others is the one that God will use for you." Luke 6:38 (GNB)

Giving is a biblical principle that has been proven to be effective over time. Giving is not God taking away from us, but the other way round. It is us letting go out of what we have to create room for more so God's blessings can come in. God said in the scriptures, 'But this I say, He which soweth sparingly shall reap also sparingly, and he which soweth bountifully shall reap also bountifully" (2 Corinthians 9:6).

Now, even in giving, there are certain standards put in place by God. One is that giving must be done in secret. God is so particular about how we give that Jesus said in Matthew 6: 2-4 that 'Therefore when you do a charitable deed, do not sound a trumpet before you as the hypocrites do in the synagogues and the streets, that they may have glory from men. Assuredly, I say to you, they have their reward. But when you do a charitable deed, do not let your left hand know what your right hand is doing, that your charitable deed may be in secret; and your Father who sees in secret will Himself reward you openly.'

Another standard put in place is that giving has to cost us. We saw this in the life of the widow that gave her last money as an offering in the scriptures (Mark 12:41-41 KJV).

5. Mentorship

"Show me a successful individual and I'll show you someone who had real positive influences in his or her life. I don't care what you do for a living—if you do it well I'm sure someone was cheering you on or showing the way. A mentor." Denzel Washington

While it is important to have a vision, a goal (either short term or long term), it is very important to have someone to look unto; someone who has passed through the same borders, who has gone through the same path or a similar path that leads to fulfilling your vision. The importance of mentorship in achieving one's vision cannot be over-emphasized. Jesus showed us the importance of mentorship (which is regarded as discipleship in the kingdom) in the scriptures by the gathering together of disciples. Jesus taught, counseled, advised, and showed the disciples what and who they are to look like and after He left; we all can see that they became like their master; JESUS.

As a believer, our first role model is Christ Jesus, The author and the finisher of our faith. He is the one we are to live after, pattern our lives after, and become like. Albeit, having discovered your God-given vision, you need to take time to carefully search for a mentor that can devote his/her time to help you fulfill your vision by offering the right counsel, providing the necessary push, and information. Just like in the scriptures, Apostle Paul said to the church in Corinth, 'Be ye followers of me, even as I also am of Christ.' (1 Cor. 11:1).

BENEFITS OF MENTORSHIP

Let us look at the role of mentorship in fulfilling your vision. Before we dive into this, let me say this; it is very important that you already know your vision and have goals before entering a mentorship program, as this will help you to streamline your search. Now, let us look at the role of mentorship in fulfilling your vision.

Of all the things mentorship offers, the first I will talk about is guidance. This is because of how important having the right counsel is. The Bible talks about this and it says 'Where no counsel is, the people fall: but in the multitude of counselors there is safety' (Pro. 11:14). Mentorship provides you a guide, a counselor, one to give you information on how to birth your vision and avoid mistakes that could mar your vision temporarily or permanently or mistakes such person has made in time past. Often, this alone has been the saving grace some men enjoyed in time past that helped them to birth their visions. Mentors also provide the how-to. Also, in their counsels, mentors offer relevant and specific information that will help you to birth your God-given vision.

Another thing I will speak on is encouragement. So many times, as men, we have dreams, passion, and vision, but we can somehow be lackadaisical about it or maybe, just maybe, in all sincerity be tired or discouraged. Mentors are the ones you run to at this stage. They will encourage you, push you and give you genuine reasons to stand and continue the race. They do this so well because, at some points in their lives, they have been there. They have been at that point where you would want to quit and give up, but they did not stop; they continued, they pushed and overcame those obstacles that wanted to deter them. So, by experience, they can tell you it is not the end; it is not the time to give up or quit and encourage you to push on. This is one of the reasons why a lot of people pay thousands of dollars per month, week or year to attend conferences just to hear someone or have someone to encourage them; a mentor.

Mentorship will also afford you having someone higher than you that you can share ideas on how to fulfill your vision with. You two can rub minds together and arrive at a great idea or a better way to by fulfilling your vision. This can be very helpful; I mean what most of us need sometimes is someone to perfect that brilliant but yet-to-be-completed idea for us. So here, having a mentor comes in.

One other thing having a mentor provides is being advocated for. This doesn't happen often in mentorship, as you and your mentor might not be co-workers; you might not even be in the same state or region. But in the rare occasion that you are colleagues, you have someone to advocate for you in your place of work.

Like I said at the beginning of this passage that in fulfilling your vision, mentorship can never be over-emphasized. So, do well to look carefully and prayerfully to choose a mentor for yourself if you do not have one already.

HOW DO YOU PICK THE RIGHT MENTOR FOR YOUR VISION?

I have spoken earlier of the importance of having the right mentor or mentorship for your vision. So, how do you go by it? I will speak briefly on this so follow me carefully.

Firstly, let us look at what the Bible has to say about having the right mentor;

'He who walks with the wise shall be wise, but a companion with fools shall be destroyed.'

-Proverbs 13:20 KJV

From the scripture passage above, you can see that the scripture is not only particular about having mentorship, but also about having the right kind of mentorship. So, how do you look and select the right mentor for yourself? Let us look into it.

The first step to take in selecting the right mentor after realizing your God-given vision is to carefully look at someone already walking in that same vision or at least a similar one. This is because for the mentorship to be effective, the mentor must possess some kind of experience to be able to offer you the right counsel and help you make informed and predictive decisions and also help you to avoid mistake(s) that he/she must have made in times past.

Another thing to look for is that the person must be approachable and easily accessible. While the person doesn't need to be in your region or locality, you must be able to reach him/her. This is important and should not be neglected.

After fulfilling the two steps above, then you make your intentions for them to be your mentor known to them most respectfully and why you would like them to be your mentor. You must be able to convince them that they will not be wasting their time by devoting much time to you.

1. Knowledge

'My people are destroyed for lack of knowledge: because thou hast rejected knowledge, I will also reject thee, that thou shalt be no priest to me: seeing thou hast forgotten the law of thy God, I will also forget thy children.'

-Hosea 4:6 KJV

Earlier, I talked about diligence. We looked at what it is and what God's word says about diligence and how important it is. Being diligent on your path to fulfilling your vision will make you seek knowledge. Knowledge is so important the lack of it can make/destroy someone. You saw in the passage of the scripture above how valuable knowledge is. God will reject a man without knowledge. The scriptures in Proverbs 24:3-4 says 'by wisdom a house is built, and by understanding it is established; by knowledge the rooms are filled with all precious and pleasant riches'. You will see here again how important knowledge is.

God will do His own by revealing to you His vision for your life, but you will have to research it to acquire adequate knowledge. You will have to give yourself to knowledge, to know what it is, to have a deep understanding of what it is, to know the people that have passed through this same route (those that succeeded and those that failed), the tools that would be needed to fulfill this vision that God Has shown you. This might cause you to search through the scriptures, pray to receive the how from The Holy Spirit, search the internet, meet some people to ask questions, and do some other things.

All these might be tiring or stressful, but you have to do them. That is where diligence comes in. During this search for knowledge, you might want to give in or stop, but a diligent heart would not rest. Diligence will tell you to keep pushing yourself till you possess enough knowledge and are saturated. One other thing that needs to be done is wrangling. There is a need to sort the knowledge acquired, to put them in order, and to get rid of ones that would not be of benefit so that true knowledge can be determined and worked with.

Now, it does not end here. After acquiring knowledge, it is very important to know how to apply this knowledge and ultimately apply it that you can fulfill your vision and achieve success. Remember, knowledge is power. Seek it.

2. Trusting in the Holy Ghost

Trusting the Holy Ghost to guide us towards a greater understanding of God's purpose for our lives is a wonderful place to start. However, this is more complicated than it appears, although, in some ways, it is not. Even intelligent theologians struggle to articulate the person of the Holy Ghost, but it is evident, particularly from the New Testament, that the Spirit is a "person" in His own right and not merely a means of stating "God is at work." What is certain is that the Holy Ghost brings honor to both the Father and the Son, and one way He accomplishes this is by revealing the Father and Son to us.

We may not be able to talk much about His "person," but we can tell so much about Him by the things He helps us see, think, talk, and do. One outstanding Christian was driven by the Spirit to argue that the only fruit produced by the Spirit is that which pleases God and reflects His character. The Spirit makes God available to us in these and other ways. He assists us in entering God's presence, not as if we're entering a room, but as a spiritual connection and friendship. And now that He has brought us into God's house and presence, He is teaching us how to be more and more at home in that place.

Some individuals don't talk about the Holy Spirit so often that you'd think they'd be OK without Him - but they can't. Others wish to talk about nothing but the Spirit, giving the appearance that there was no Father or Son - this is not the case. (And a lot of the time, they're not talking about the Spirit; they're talking about themselves.)

The good news is that our lack of understanding of the Spirit's "person," or the fact that we either ignore or push Him ahead of the Father and Son, does not prevent Him from acting on our behalf. He continues to glorify the Father and Son; He continues to enlighten our eyes, develop our faith, and enrich our lives in holiness. The truth is that He doesn't mind not having "center stage." Christ dispatched Him as a "strengthener" and counselor, saying, "He will not speak on his own... He will bring me honor." (Matthew 16:13-14) That is the Holy Spirit for you; sent from the Father and eager to honor the Father's Son via instruction, transformation, and sanctification of people.

We intend to indicate that the Spirit isn't bothered by our ignoring Him. He surely does, for excluding Him closes doors and slows progress in connection with God. The Spirit is merciless because He is fully and continuously hostile to the evil inside and around us as written in Galatians 5:17. This indicates He is serious about bringing God and us together, and we can trust Him to get us there.

CHAPTER 6

BY WISDOM

"The Lord BY wisdom made the earth, BY understanding, HE made the heavens"

- Proverbs 4:5-6

From my childhood, there is this question that has always bothered me and that question is this: "Why does the sky not fall?" Seeing how vast and endless it looks, seeing that it stretches from one end of the horizon to the other, I used to be confused as to what holds it. At times I'll be like: "what holds the sky" is there any time it can fall?" Seeing that every other thing I see is fixed to something, I'm surprised how the sky stands on its own.

Trees are connected to stems and roots, heads are attached to the neck and other playlets of the body, but where is the sky attached? I soon figured out what holds the sky. It is the same thing that keeps the fishes in the sea and not in the desert; it is these same things that but keep the ground and not heads. What then is this things? That thing, I found out is the Wisdom of God.

Have you ever wondered what would have happened if the creator of the whole universe didn't do things to precision? Let me give you a little bit of insight to that. In our solar system, the earth is the third planet with relation to proximity to the sun, that is, the earth is the third closest planet to the sun. What would've happened if earth and Venus were to switch places? If earth goes closer to the sun, it will be too hot and inhabitable.

What if the earth goes farther from the sun, if the earth goes farther from the sun, green house effects will decrease and we might as well go back to the ice age. Which cause the extinction of many organisms we have now. Seeing the destruction that can happen by based on a little shift in earth's position makes me convinced that God indeed is a perfect designer.

This perfection through which God made everything is the wisdom of God. God is so wise that he understands what every organism needs to survive its habitat. While human beings breathe with noses and lungs, fishes breathe with gills. While, human beings breathe in Oxygen and exhale Carbon dioxide, plants breathe in carbon dioxide and breathe in Oxygen for us to use. Did you see the wisdom in that design?

Yes, that is God's wisdom. The Bible verse quoted above affirms that God made the earth by wisdom and the heavens by understanding, in order words; the currency for creation is wisdom and understanding. The creative power of God is one of the things that make him God and that creative power is manifested in wisdom. In this chapter I would expose to you how wisdom is important in finding your purpose and walking in it. However before I do that let me run you through the different kinds of wisdom we have around today.

KINDS OF WISDOM

One of the downsides of good things is that they always have a counterfeit. No matter how exclusive they are there will be a fake and substandard version of it. Although the wisdom of God is perfect and imperative, there's another form of wisdom flying around today that most people run after neglecting the divine and infallible wisdom of God.

The first type of wisdom I'll talk about is the wisdom of the world. The Bible talks about this kind of wisdom in the book of James 3: 14-16 *"But if you have bitter envy and self-seeking in your hearts, do not boast and lie against the truth. This wisdom does not descend from above, but is earthly, sensual, demonic. For where envy and self-seeking exist, confusion and every evil thing are there."*

From the Bible verses quoted above, we can see the attributes and definition of the worldly wisdom. This form of wisdom is never in tandem with the truth. As a matter of fact, it is designed to speak against the truth. I would discuss with you some of the attributes of this wisdom.

1. Envy and Selfishness: This form of wisdom is designed to advance self. Hence, it is envious of others. When you start to notice that you get uncomfortable with other people's good, when you start getting offending at your friend's progress or you feel you are in a better position for success that the person that succeeded, beware, it is the sign of worldly wisdom. When everything you have and everything you want is all about you, then your life is being structured and governed by worldly wisdom.

2. Boasting and Falsehood: It is a disaster today that our world systems have made it look like God is the problem of the world. In politics, sports, entertainment, finance and even religion; we are gradually relegating God to the back seat. Anyone that dares mention God's name and stand by it is tagged a fanatic: this is the wisdom of the world! It always boasts of itself and never gives glory to God. Little wonder we see people run to science for answer and leave Hid at the by-stands. If you will go far with your God given purpose then you must be careful not to pattern your life after he wisdom of the world. How can the maker of the world be the problem of the world?

3. Earthly and Sensual: This form of wisdom is earthly and sensual, this means that it conforms to rules of men. Given that all men are imperfect, this kind of wisdom is imperfect. It is sensual because, it does not only permits sin, it also sponsors it. This form of wisdom makes don look therapeutic and harmless. It legalises abortion, it normalises adultery and fornication, it qualifies lies and cheating, this wisdom permits anarchy and disobedience.

4. Demonic: Sin always attracts demons and because this form of wisdom allows sin and sponsors it, it is demonic. This implies that, any life that operates this form of wisdom will be tormented by demons. No wonder most of the worldly wise men die of terrible things God's wisdom is a solution for. Yes, because they do not know that the "joy of the Lord is a source of strength," they die in depression. They do not know there is "a more abundant life" they die in their lacks, confusions and sins. What a shame!

Having considered the wisdom of the world and how it operates, I will now explain to you the wisdom of God and how it relates to your purpose in life. In the same James Chapter 3, the Bible says in verses 17-18 that, *"the wisdom that is from above is first pure, then peaceable, gentle, willing to yield, full of mercy and good fruits, without partiality and without hypocrisy. Now the fruit of righteousness is sown in peace by those who make peace."*

As a sharp contrast to the many imperfections and destructive tendencies of the wisdom of this world, James explains to us the wonders of God's wisdom, let's examine it more closely.

1. It is first pure: The first notable thing about the wisdom that comes from God is that it is pure. According to the Merriam Webster's dictionary, to be pure is to be free from stain and dirt: spotless. It is no more news that Christians live in a world of contaminants, you no longer need to leave your house or pay money to sin against God. Sin has been made easy.

However, the first thing you need to maintain God's kind of wisdom is purity.. This includes mental purity (where your thoughts and imaginations are pure), sexual purity (abstinence from fornication, adultery and other immoral acts), relational purity (being in peace with all men and wanting the best for them) and behavioural purity (purity in your character and conducts).

2. Peaceable and gentle: If the wisdom you carry is from God, one of the first things it will teach you is being gentle and peaceful. Peace is not the absence of trouble but the ability to maintain tranquility in the midst of the storms. The wisdom of God exposes you to His promises and this helps you to remains calm and gentle in the midst of all problems and situations.

3. Willing to yield: God is not a rebel! If truly you are a child of God and you seek to walk in the realm of His perfect wisdom, then you must be willing to conform to His laws; you must conform to His own person and become Him. God's plan is not to raise men who are independent of Him, no! His plan is to raise men that live perfectly because they depend on Him for all. Hence, you must learn to submit fully to God's will, His ways and His plans.

4. Full of Mercy and Good fruits: In Matthew 5:18-20, the Bible says that "A good tree cannot bear bad fruit, nor *can* a bad tree bear good fruit. Every tree that does not bear good fruit is cut down and thrown into the fire. Therefore by their fruits you will know them." Jesus Christ already explained what it means to carry the wisdom of God.

Wisdom is not silent or redundant; it speaks, it is to be seen, it is meant to produce, to create and to organise. Hence, the kinds of things you produce will show to the world the kind of wisdom you operate. God will never give you wisdom that will provide fruits that dishonour His name. If it is God that inspired you, your products will glorify His name.

Asides providing fruits that glorify the name of God, the wisdom that comes from God is merciful. That is to say that, it helps the needy. The needy doesn't only mean the poor. The wisdom from God preaches the gospel to the broken hearted; it liberates the captive, it blesses the poor and encourages the downcast! God's wisdom is relevant in building lives, not destroying it.

5. Without Partiality, without hypocrisy: The last thing the Bible says about the wisdom of God is that it's not partial, neither is it hypocritical. It's to a governor what it is to a servant. And this comes to play in the decision making process of an individual. If you are controlled by God's wisdom, your decision will be apt, direct and without any form of partiality or hypocrisy.

Having understood the difference between the wisdom that comes from God and the worldly kind of wisdom, it is imperative I explain to you how one can access the wisdom of God. At some points in everyone's life; they have identified a need to be helped by God. They've seen the need to manoeuvre through situations by bee wisdom; however, the problem is not knowing God's wisdom but accessing it and applying it for one's benefit.

HOW TO ACCESS GOD'S WISDOM

1. Desire it: In Proverbs 4:6-7, the Bible says that *"you should not forsake wisdom, and she will preserve you; Love her, and she will keep you. Wisdom is the principal thing; therefore get wisdom. And in all your getting, get understanding."* The tone of this passages sounds like a love letter for wisdom. It appears that anyone that will experience the wisdom of God must desire it like a new groom desires his wife.

There must be a consistent longing, a continuous hunger and an unending need for wisdom. It is only those who hunger and thirst that would be filled. Knowing that wisdom is the principal thing—it is important for every life that will be creative and successful—one can start seeking it with seriousness and consistency.

2. Ask God for it: After you've seen the great need for wisdom, the best step is to ask the One who owns it. The Bible says in James 1:5 that anyone who lacks wisdom should ask from God who gives it generously.

Did you see that? Ask God, not men. You can't ask your biology teacher for God's wisdom and expect to be answered. If it belongs to God, only Him can give it. God's wisdom is not a jewel to be won for being holy or astoundingly prayerful; it is a gift God decides to give to anyone that asks Him diligently. What are you waiting for, set the prayer wheel rolling and ask your Father for wisdom.

3: Study the word of God: In John 1:1, the Bible says in the beginning was the Word and the Word was with God and the Word was God. This shows that the Word of God does not just tell us about God; it is God personified. The Word of God is not just another literature written about God but it is the person of God, the nature of God and the life of God.

In the same vein, 1 Corinthians 1:24 says that Christ is the Power and Wisdom of God, and seeing that Christ Who is the Word of God is also the wisdom of God, it is important that you become accustomed to the Word of God if you will possess the wisdom of God.

When you study the Bible with an open and receptive heart, you are not engaging another work of literature nor are you reading a book written by several authors. You are simply accessing the Life of Christ encoded on every page of the scripture. Bible study is the Christian's only way of downloading instructions from God.

You must understand that everything a man needs to access God's wisdom and apply it to every area of his life has been revealed in the scriptures. You might want to ask me like others do, "Why then do I study the Bible and do not understand?" The answer is not far-fetched: anything God has coded only Him can decipher it.

God encoded His instructions, life and power in the Bible and leaves it to you to search them out. Simply put, God uploaded all the secrets of His wisdom into a database (the Bible) and gave that database to men, but they need a code to access it. This code is what you need to access God's wisdom. Are you interested in knowing what that code is? Then follow me to the next point.

4. Allow the Spirit of God to lead you: The spirit of God is the code that helps you unlock mysteries from the word of God. The difference between the revealed word of God and the letters we see in the Bible is the breath of the Spirit. When you allow the spirit of God to breathe instruction into in while studying the Bible, you will be able to access God's wisdom.

Interestingly, the spirit of God does not only reveal the Bible to you, it also helps you to obey it. Given that the wisdom of God is far from that of men, most people find it difficult to comprehend it and submit to it. This is where the Holy Spirit comes in; He conforms you to the patterns of God's wisdom.

Let's see what the Bible says in Acts 10:38; the Bible speaks of how God anointed Jesus with the Holy Ghost and with Power. When God seeks to empower a man with wisdom or any other virtue, He does not give him things first; He gives him the Holy Ghost. You see, a man can only be as relevant to God as He submits to God's Spirit.

5. Study to show yourself approved: There is a dimension of wisdom that is given to men by God, but that is not all here is to wisdom. When God gifts you wisdom, it is not a superpower that automatically makes you learned or wise. Rather, it is a supernatural ability to 'know' and 'understand' without limitations. Hence, there is a need for you to study. One of the things that baffle me about Christ is the relevance of His messages.

When you consider the depth and diversity of His parables, you will know that asides the fact that He is the Wisdom of God, He is a versatile reader. His parables include depth in agriculture, astronomy, mathematics and language. He even demonstrates a deep knowledge in history, politics and religion, what more?

Daniel is another man the Bible talks about. Daniel studied a lot that he was learned in all the sciences and philosophies of one of the most sophisticated empires in history: the Babylonian Empire. The men that possess the wisdom of God are not nonentities; they are professionals who are so verse that none can refute the wisdom of God in them.

Do not forget, wisdom is also knowledge in action, so there is a place of knowing. The question then is this: what do you know? While you study the laws and ways of God through the Bible, it is important you also increase your knowledge and versatility while allowing God's spirit to help you discern what and what not to learn. When God announces you by wisdom to your generation, it is only your own foolishness that can bring you down, so learn to Learn!

GOD'S WISDOM, YOUR VISION AND PURPOSE

Having considered the types of wisdom and how to access it, it is therefore imperative to see how the wisdom one acquires from God and learns can be used to cultivate one's vision and purpose. It has been mentioned earlier in this book that vision and purpose are important for a successful life in God. Hence, in this section I'll bring you practical ways through which God's wisdom can benefit your life by helping you catch a vision about your purpose and actualise it.

As discussed earlier, God's wisdom is revealed by Him through His word by the help of the Holy Spirit. Hence, the first thing the wisdom of God gives you is perspective and focus. In a world of so many 'technological advancements' here are so many things that battles for a man's attention. This is why a man that has allowed himself to be exposed to God's word learns to focus and stay disciplined.

Let's consider Joseph for instance. He has a vision about his purpose, he already knows where God is taking him, but then, the devil organised pitfalls to truncate his destiny. However, because his perspective is not shaped by the wisdom of the world but by the wisdom of God which is divine, he fled from the temptation that would've ended his destiny.

Come to think of it, everyone in Joseph's shows could have considered falling for Potiphar's wife; she was beautiful, rich, connected and influential. If Joseph had succumbed to her, she could have planned a coup with him to kill her husband and connected Joseph to where he would get a good job, but the best Joseph would have being would have been "master of Potiphar's house."

However, Joseph understands through God's wisdom that sin is always a reducing agent. Sun is meant to reduce man's destiny. This perspective Joseph has gained through God's wisdom helped him to stay on track. He knows that the wisdom that is from above is pure.

Another advantage of God's Wisdom in relation to your purpose is that it gives you divine enablement. The wisdom of is not only a catalogue of DIYs or tutorials; it is an empowerment for success. Do not forget that Christ is the Power and Wisdom of God. There is no person who lives based on God's wisdom and direction that ends up as a weakling. Though your beginning may be small, if you stay on the dictates of God's wisdom, it empowers you for the top!

Let's consider the life of Daniel. Daniel was one of the young boys that were brought to Babylon as "casualties of war" from Judaea. He was a young boy in a strange land where his human rights or opinion did not matter. He could be cheated, molested, injured or even killed by the lowest ranking soldier in Babylon, but God through His wisdom empowered Daniel for the top.

He troubled the king with a dream and when there was an audition for wise men, Daniel qualified as one of the wise men in the whole Babylonian empire. What a great wisdom! Soon, his life was threatened by a decree to do something that had never been done before. He was to reveal and interpret a dream the king forgot. This was a challenge that seemed insurmountable.

As a matter of fact, no science in the 21st century can do that. Our genetics, psychology, metaphysics, and even logic will fail at this task. Daniel came to an end of his abilities; what did he do? He ran to God and he received empowerment. The dream was revealed alongside its interpretation and Daniel was promoted.

One thing about the wisdom of God is that it begins where your capabilities end. God's wisdom is a divine empowerment that does not need a man's goodness or brilliance. You must understand that although any man that carries God's wisdom will be wise, it is not brilliance. Brilliance is logical, while God's wisdom is supernatural. Brilliance is empirical and limited, while God's wisdom is divine and limitless.

Another important thing to note about God's wisdom in relation to your purpose is that it creates. God's wisdom is creative. It makes beauty from ashes, gowns of gladness from robes of mourning and success from failure. The fact that you are following God's wisdom and doing His will does not mean that challenges will not come, no! Challenges will surely come, but God's wisdom teaches you to creatively turn challenges to chances and situations to solutions.

One time, while Jesus was having a camp meeting in the wilderness, people were hungry and couldn't take the long walk back home if they didn't eat something. This was a serious issue. If Jesus were to send his disciples to go and get food from the nearest city there would be no money enough. In fact, it will be difficult for them to transport food for 5,000 people without a big car.

If Jesus dismissed the people to go and buy food themselves, they could die by the way. This would have generated a great scandal towards His ministry. Jesus simply applied the wisdom of God and manufactured endless food from 5 loaves of bread and 2 fishes. What an audacity! What a different level of operation!

Are you currently going through a time in your life when it seems life your visions are getting blurred? Does it seem like what you have is insufficient to achieve your purpose? What you need is God's wisdom. If He can found the earth upon the seas through wisdom and stretch out the skies without a foundation; then there is something in Him that would help you achieve your purpose and actualise your vision.

CHAPTER 7

STICK WITH YOUR TESTED WEAPON

"Any weapon is a good weapon as long as ye can use it with honor and skill"

- Brian Jacques

Have you ever wondered why people tend to succeed more in what they love doing? Do you ever think of how they achieve their goals quickly? The answer to this is that they are original and understand what God has placed in their hands and are executing them correctly. There are time in life when it seems like what you're doing is not enough, it seems like you are the only person around who is not making progress, like everything you're doing is a mistake. As bad as this may be, it is not a time to start trying to be someone else or giving up on yourself.

Our world is one where fake things gain more prominence than originals. When you go on social media you will see people flaunt their new cars, their new deals, their new businesses, their new converts and all, but here you are trying to make sense of your situation. Should you just abandon your vision and do what others are doing? Wouldn't it be a logical solution to start doing what everybody does so as to have what everybody has? As logical as this seems, it is not true. The popular solution is not always the best solution. And have you asked yourself this: "If I leave my unique purpose to follow what everyone else is doing, who will achieve my goal?"

The actual plan of God for you is to succeed. He made this known in the book of Jeremiah 29:11 (KJV), which says, *"For I know the thoughts that I think toward you, saith the LORD, thoughts of peace, and not of evil, to give you an expected end."* This is why He imbedded in you a weapon with which you can use to succeed. We all have different purposes in life and God gives every one of us unique tools and instruments to achieve these purposes. We cannot all be good singers; we can't all be good analyst or good planners. That does not mean what you are good at is bad.

WHAT IS IN YOUR HAND?

"And the LORD said unto him, what is that in thine hand? And he said, a rod."

- Exodus 4:2 (KJV)

Everyone has a weapon that's been configured according to the way they were created by God. Merriam Webster's thesaurus defines a weapon as a person or thing used to produce a result. In other words, your weapon is that thing that belongs to you, and when you use it effectively, it'll create whatever outcome you desire. Unfortunately, most times, it is 'inactive' – unnoticed and unused until some life situation brings it forward, then you realize that you have this concealed capacity or talent that you had known nothing about.

In this context, the weapon being discussed is that God had ordained you with, placed in your hands that you may use to achieve those goals he has given to you. However, you can't achieve this correctly if you don't know what your weapon is. The ignorance of it might even make you use other people's weapons with the thought that it will work for you. Looking at the story of David in the Bible, when he wanted to fight Goliath, the Philistine, King Saul gave him his armor and sword, but because the weapon wasn't his, he couldn't use it. (1 Samuel 17: 39).

Another example was Moses, in the book of Exodus when the Lord God called him to be a deliverer unto the children of Israel, but then he doubted his capacity, and then God asked him Exodus 4:2 (KJV) *"And the LORD said unto him, what is that in thine hand? And he said, A rod."* This is where God made him realize that he already had a weapon that would help achieve the task He had given to him. If you read further, you will see that he kept using that weapon (Rod) to do amazing things among the Israelites.

You'll ask me; how do I know my weapon? Of course, you can't just recognize it that easily. Although just like Moses, you might not know what is in your hands or what your weapon might be until someone helps you realize it. That is why you must walk closely with God and maintain a relationship with Him so that He will open your eyes to see this weapon.

Like the success story I shared earlier, the CEO never knew what was in her hand. She had no idea that the simple recipe she learned was enough to yield more profit until God revealed it to her.

The ignorance of what you have in your hand or what your weapon is could make you find it hard to achieve your goal, and you might use other people's weapons with the thought that it'll work out for you. And just so you know, that's a very wrong assumption because it might not turn out that way, that's why there are some steps to follow:

1. Develop a relationship with God

The first step you should take is to make sure there is a close relationship between you and God. For example, David was bold enough to face the lion and the boar that came to attack his sheep in the bush because the spirit of God was with him.. He could kill them with his bare hands because the Lord was with him. Another example is Joseph in the Bible.

At first, he never knew who kept revealing those visions and dreams to him, and he never knew the interpretation until the Lord made him understand it. Eventually, God revealed the understanding to him, which was the weapon that helped him get a seat at the top position in Egypt. There are several other examples of men in the Bible who walked with God closely and knew their weapons. Therefore, it is essential that you walk closely with God; the relationship between you and Him will help you see and understand that weapon in your hand.

2. Maintain That Relationship with God

This is a very integral part. You can't just plant a seed and then leave it all by itself. No! You'll have to water it and nurture it until it is fully grown and ready to bear fruit. That's how it is when you're in a relationship with God; you must make sure it is continuously developed without anything disrupting it.

You must be wondering, how do I go about this? That's easy. What you'll do is to first, make sure you always meditate on His word daily just like the book of Joshua chapter 1:8 "This book of the law shall not depart out of thy mouth, but thou shalt meditate therein day and night…" The word of God is a guide to your whole being; it reveals to you, the steps to take and directs you in line with the will of God.

The book of Psalm 119:105 (KJV) says *"Thy word is a lamp unto my feet, and a light unto my path."* The word of God lights the way ahead of you so you can see vividly which way to go. So then, through every season of your life, you can be confident that God is always leading you through His Word. More so, when you study the word of God, you'll be able to pray according to His will and have the confidence that He hears you.

3. Pray continually

This is another essential step you should take. You must continuously seek God's face by praying; it is direct means of communication to God. The book of 1Thessalonians 5:17 (KJV) says *"pray without ceasing,"* which means you need to pray continually; it aligns you to the thought God has for you and provides answers that you need. Matthew 7:7 (KJV) says, *"Ask, and it shall be given you; seek, and ye shall find; knock, and it shall be opened unto you:"* So God has given us full assurance that anytime we ask anything we will surely be given.

4. Search within yourself

You should search deep within yourself, take your time to sit and think about your whole being, what you find yourself doing with ease, and with the leading of the spirit of God, you'll find that weapon that God has designed for you specifically. Your weapon is that talent, gift, virtue, idea that comes to you naturally, and when you do it or use it, it's effortless and comfortable. It is something 'immanent' – it is a part of you, you enjoy doing it, you're good at it, and it makes you feel accomplished and fulfilled.

USE YOUR WEAPON

"Then he that had received the five talents went and traded with the same, and made them other five talents."
- Matthew 25:16 (KJV)

Have you discovered your weapon? What next? Very simple—make use of it appropriately. God has ordained the weapon in you and in your hands—no matter how insignificant it is—to execute it properly and use it to achieve that purpose He wants you to fulfill. He didn't implant it in you so that it'll be dormant, never! But rather so that it will yield fruit as well as be a blessing to others around you.

So you shouldn't be like the unfaithful servant in the book of Matthew chapter 25 verse 22 who was given one talent but hid it instead of using it appropriately for his master. But rather be like the other servant who had thought it wise to use his talent and got additional five talents for his master.

A man of God once said, *"If God wanted the woods to be quiet, He would not have given birds songs to sing."* In other words, if God didn't want you to execute that weapon, He wouldn't implant it in you at creation. So, therefore, you mustn't allow this weapon to remain dormant and become blunt that it cannot be used again. How would you execute this weapon, you'd ask? But, then, after you must have known your weapon, there are things you must understand and do to make use of your weapon correctly. They have been listed below:

THE PURPOSE OF YOUR WEAPON

The moment you've discovered your weapon, the first thing you should understand is the purpose of the weapon you have. Like I mentioned earlier, the relationship you've developed with God will help you understand this purpose easily. For example, David, at first, did not know why God allowed him to kill that lion and bear that attacked his Father's sheep. It was when he got to the camp of the Israelites that he realized that the Lord had made him strong so that he would defeat a more potent enemy as well as be a tool in His Hands and a means of help to God's people.

The same thing with Joseph; he never understood the interpretation of his dream until he came to Egypt and God revealed it to him. This shows that every weapon has a purpose and each purpose can only be made understood by the spirit of God. Nevertheless, the primary purpose of every God-ordained weapon is to benefit others, glorify God, and fulfill your God-given purpose. Let this be noted in your heart.

1. Cultivate it

Since you've known the "why" of your designed weapon, the next step is to cultivate it.

For a planted seed to germinate and bear good fruit, it needs to be well taken care of. Therefore, cultivating your ordained weapon involves observing, developing, and nurturing it.

When you observe your weapon, you relate its presence to your physical body, for instance, know what you need to sacrifice or do without in order to use it effectively, and you should connect it also with your environment. Indeed, there will be something in your environment that requires that weapon. Then you develop it by studying it and learning more about it. This will help you become an excellent steward and will also make that weapon work effectively.

2. Test it

Testing your weapon implies practicing it and consciously applying it to your daily activities. Owning the weapon isn't enough; you should learn to exercise it as well. Do not be afraid to branch out! It is a weapon that has been ordained in you by God to help you achieve goals, so why should you be frightened? The Bible made us understand that David wasn't able to use Saul's Armor just because he hadn't tested it, but then he picked up his sling and stones because he had that confidence that if God could deliver the lion and bear into his hands, then who was Goliath before Him (1Samuel 17: 36).

The prophet Moses was no exception; having tested the weapon in his hand in the presence of God, he wasn't afraid to do so in the presence of Pharaoh the king of Egypt (Exodus 7: 10-12), and of course, we know the outcome. So if you have this same confidence that this weapon in your hands is what you'll use to achieve your desired goal, then why don't you exercise it and see what amazing things you could do with it. Therefore, it is vital to practice and continually labor to improve your weapon, so don't get caught up in wishful thinking. Instead, develop a habit of exercising your weapon.

3. Be the Master!

The Bible tells us in the book of Proverb 22:29 (KJV), *"Seest thou a man diligent in his business? he shall stand before kings;*

he shall not stand before mean men." This means when you are the master of your weapon, you can stand before great men and do amazing things.

Becoming the master of your craft (weapon) means getting comprehensive knowledge or being more skilled in it. This is a vital part of executing your weapon. First, you have to get the hang of it; understand it! Know more. Don't just say "well, I already know what it is, so there's no need to be serious about it." No, that's not right. You need to focus on it and understand it better because it will lead you into a deeper connection with yourself and others.

This shows that being a master takes a great deal of time, effort, and desire, and requires continuous action and persistent intensity. The reason you need to master your weapon is so that it will be used extraordinarily. If you leave your weapon without adding more knowledge or improving it, you might become mediocre, and it will only become stagnant and ordinary. Nothing special, nothing excellent.

This reminds me of the story of a young man who was very skilled in drawing. It was something he was good at and had people amazed at whatever he drew. However, he felt too comfortable with himself because people were still commenting on his minor works. He felt that was 'all' and that there was no need to improve his skills.

Little did he know that when you don't continue to nurture a plant, it dies gradually. And so little by little, this talent began to fade. Finally, reality hit him hard when he saw his friend who had the same drawing skill as he wins a prize and collects an award as the best artist in the town.

The above story tells us that your ordained weapon can't stand alone; you have to add excellence to it, gain more knowledge, and harness it into something extraordinary. This will make it more effective. When you improve your experience, you improve your growth!

ORDINARY YET EXTRAORDINARY

"Did this because Daniel, the one the king named Belteshazzar, was found to have an extraordinary spirit, knowledge, and perception, and the ability to interpret dreams, explain riddles, and solve problems. Therefore, summon Daniel, and he will give the interpretation."

- Daniel 5:12 (NET)

Yes, your ordained weapon might look ordinary, but then there is no limitation to making it extraordinary. For example, Daniel was just an ordinary Hebrew youth but had an extraordinary spirit which made the King of Babylon seek him every time he needed to understand that unusual dream. So when you use innovative methods to execute your weapon, it produces extraordinary results. And this innovation can only come when you've become the master of your craft.

The comprehensive knowledge you've acquired helps you to be creative. Creativity is essential to executing your weapon. Do not get stuck because you feel it's something you're comfortable with when you use it. Instead, try out other ways and learn new ways with which you can use your weapon.

Again, take David's sling and stone, for instance. He knew he could use that as a powerful weapon to defeat Goliath as long as God was with him. This shows that you definitely need the wisdom of God to try new things. But then, to be creative, you need to let go of fear, abandon what you already know, and take the courage to push for something new.

Hence, having done all these, executing your weapon correctly shouldn't be a challenging task. And the way you choose to do it solely depends on you, not the opinion of any other person.

YOU'VE GOTTEN IT. STICK TO IT!

"David strapped his sword on his clothing, and he tried to move; for he had not tested it. David said to Saul, "I can't go with these; for I have not tested them." David took them off."

- 1 Samuel 17: 39

The weapon is known already, and you've begun to use it for that God-given Goal; now you have to stick it. Although the vision might look hazy at first and uneasy to carry out, do not fret because God is with you; he will lead you and take you to your destination.

Do not try to use others' opinions to execute your vision. What works for Mr. A might not work for Mr. B. we all have different configurations according to God's creation. Therefore stick to the weapon God has designed for you because it will work for you exceptionally. You don't have to do what others are doing.

Despite how equipped and protective Saul's armor was, David could make use of it because he hadn't tested it, and that wasn't the weapon God designed for him. Another man who stuck to his Weapon was Daniel. The King of Babylon needed young men who had good knowledge, were intelligent, good-looking, and wise.

So he instructed his princes to feed the servants and the Hebrews, who were his captives. But the Bible made us understand in the book of Daniel (NIV) chapter 1:8 *"But Daniel resolved not to defile himself with the royal food and wine, and he asked the chief official for permission not to defile himself this way."*

So Daniel decided to stick to the weapon he had tested, the natural food of the Hebrews. When we read further, we discovered that Daniel and his friends were ten times better than the king's servants, and the Lord also enriched him with more wisdom, knowledge, and understanding (Daniel 1:17).

Some steps would help you ensure to stick to that weapon:

1. Be Original

Jeremiah 1:5 (ESV) says, "Before I formed you in the womb I knew you, and before you were born I consecrated you; I appointed you a prophet to the nations." This means everyone has their unique ability, as God had made them. You have your own as well, so you should be who you are.

To be original here means being yourself, not copying the tactics of another person but utilizing what God has designed for you to be original also means to be uniquely different from everyone else and making use of your weapon in your time and field.

It also implies being creative with something fresh and uncommon. You should be original, be creative with your tested weapon, and do something that stands out.

2. Don't Compare

"Not that we dare to classify or compare ourselves with some of those who are commending themselves. But when they measure themselves by one another and compare themselves with one another, they are without understanding." 1 Corinthians 10:12 (ESV)

Many Christians make this type of mistake frequently. They start to compare themselves to others when it looks as if their goal can't be easily achieved. And they fail to remember that God had created them differently. Do not join that category. Whatever happens, learn not to compare yourself with others.

Comparison can clip your wings and limit you to using your God-ordained weapon to achieve your purpose. It will kill your motivation and take away your confidence. And then you find yourself doubting if the weapon in your hands can actually work. God won't want you to compare yourself or try to do it the way other people do. If that's what he wanted, he wouldn't have designed you differently.

If David had compared his sling and stones to Saul's weapon, he might not have defeated Goliath in the Bible. Instead, he believed that his weapon through God would give him victory (1 Samuel 17: 37).

An anonymous Scholar once said, *"Do what works for you. You don't have to be Michael Jordan; you just have to do what you're comfortable with."* When you don't compare yourself to others, you'll be able to stick to your weapon!

3. Believe!

"And Jesus said to him, "'If You can?' All things are possible to him who believes" Mark 9:23.

The attitude of the phrase "I believe" in you is an open path for you to truly stick to your weapon. Because when you believe that it will work out according to how the Lord had ordained you, you have no difficulty fulfilling your goal. To believe means to trust fully without any second thoughts. It is the first foundation you must build yourself on. So first, you must believe in God who gave you this weapon, believe in his ability to help you do amazing things with this weapon, and then believe in yourself. Believe in your ability; have belief in the capacity of your weapon. All these will help you stick to your weapon and help you utilize it correctly.

Moses believed, and with the weapon in his hands, he achieved his God-given purpose. Likewise, David had the confidence that God was with him, and with the weapon in his hands, he defeated Goliath. Daniel and his friends also believed that's why he was able to stick to his weapon. So you see, having the attitude of "I believe" helps you stay focused on your weapon and make you see ways to utilize it effectively. If you follow all these steps, you'll surely stick to your weapon and use it magnificently!

Finally, dearest, always know that your configuration and your designed weapon are different from others. Please get rid of the impression that what might work for others would work for you because that isn't right. Everyone has their own unique ability. You find yours, develop it, master it and use it creatively. Above all, just like the Bible book of Psalm chapter 37:5 (KJV) says, *"commit thy way unto the LORD; trust also in him; and he shall bring it to pass."*

Do not forget to commit all your plans, thoughts, and ideas into God's hands, and He will bring it to pass.

CHAPTER 8
THERE IS MORE

"One of the major keys to success is to keep moving forward on the journey, making the best of the deters and interruptions, turning adversity into advantage."
- John c. Maxwell

Linda looked stunned, as she knelt beside the lifeless body of Joshua. She couldn't believe what her eyes were seeing. She had tried everything in her reach to sustain him, even the mouth-to-mouth respiration she was advised to use. Yet, all to no avail. He was gone. Never was she going to see her cute grandson again. It seemed all like a nightmare. Was someone going to wake her up? Doesn't it amaze you how quickly what gives us joy yesterday could suddenly become the reason for sorrow today?

Five months ago, Linda had, in the labor room, watched her daughter Tanya welcomed Joshua into the world. Everyone was excited and happy, especially Linda who was honored to have her first grandchild. She felt on top of the world. In fact, minutes to the tragic death of Joshua, everyone had gone on a date, only to come home to find little Joshua dead.

Here is the point. This isn't just a tragic tale to stir up some pity in you. Rather, it's a pencil I intend to use to inscribe in your heart the fact that success can be short-lived if proper plans aren't made for its sustainability. Major manage to get to the pick of their career and get satisfied with no hope to get better and break new grounds to erect flags of new victories.

After every success, reflection and *"there is more"* mentality MUST be cultivated and sustained. To be successful and keep being successful, you mustn't keep your eyes on past successes. Beyond the conception of your vision and its actualization, there's need to be tutored on its sustainability. Come to think of it, would a mother after knowing that she had conceived a baby in her womb stop there? No! She enrolls for the ante-natal care, takes the necessary meal to get herself fit and the baby wrapped in her womb strong.

After conception comes delivery; and after delivery comes nurturing and tending! Many people's successes are like Linda's precious son—Joshua—who brings joy one moment but soon vanishes into nothing. The greatest enemy of sustained impact and success is the last ground of success we've conquered. Hence, for every child born, there must be corresponding care that sustains and keep the baby alive.

Benjamin franklin once said that *"without continual growth and progress, such words as improvement, achievement and success have no meaning."* Success itself carries with it the characteristics of continuity and progress. I have found that people often break limits and get to the peak of their endeavor, only to come crashing down a few years later, some even a few months. You must understand that God's desire for the believer isn't that you'll shine bright today and tomorrow get dim by the challenges and commitment that comes with success. This intention of God towards the believer is express in the book of Jeremiah chapter 29 and verse 11 that *"for I know the thoughts that I have toward you says the lord, thoughts of peace, and not for calamity, to give you a future and a hope"*.

Often, I see people offer sacrifices of blame and complaint to God when failure comes visiting, after a season of successes. God isn't the reason why you fall and rise on the path of fulfillment.

THE THREE CHAPTERS

You must understand that in the writing of your success story, you have three chapters. The first chapter entails that moment where you conceive your God-given vision. You are armed with the vision ready to embark on the mission of destiny fulfillment. This was the stage where Joseph's destiny was revealed to him in the dream.

The second chapter is the birthing stage, where the vision is beginning to become like it. You have the feeling of fulfillment in your life. Your story is just starting. You begin to enjoy the proceeds of the new born purpose and idea.

The third chapter, surprisingly, has no end. It's the phase of sustaining the success you have acquired and acquiring. This is the chapter where many author fail in the building of their success story. Believers lack the facilities necessary to sustain and keep the plot of their success story on.

People relax at this chapter. "This is the last chapter after all", they say. Little do they know that the irony of the chapter of sustenance is that **there is more!** Here, the end is just the beginning.

FEED AND FEED WELL!

WHO Report has it that 300 children in the United States die every hour, approximately, 2.6 million children every year, due to poor nutrition and imbalances in their diet. As many parents are negligent in the feeding of their wards, so also are many vision-bearer negligent in the nurturing, care and feeding of their God-given vision. Remember that *vision is the source and hope of life.* When you see your vision as a life and being that cannot stand the test of time, if not fed well, you wouldn't hesitate to nurture it well. How you forage your vision determine on how last it can stand the test of time and men. Do you feed your vision? Christian rise and fall in the fulfillment of their purpose, owing to inadequacy or negligence to have their vision fed or fed well.

Well, of course, I didn't mean to feed on proteins or some Chinese food full of fats and oil. Just as foods are generally categorized under eight classes, so also there are three nutrients success feeds on to be sustained and nourished. They are what I would like to call the *THREE-Vs* – Value, Virtue and Valor. To be a Christian with sustainable success, you need to be balanced in all and deficient in none of these success nutrients. A man with value but no virtue is like a child suffering from kwashiorkor. Okay, let get down to digging the treasures in these nutrients.

1. Value

Value is the degree of importance given to something. It is the quality that renders something desirable or valuable. One of what you should add to yourself is value. Add to yourself a great degree of importance. You will begin to get your star dim the moment you begin to lose value. Mind you, things that are common do not usually have much value. Furnish yourself to a degree where you seem to be the only option. One of the ways you can do this is to make that great weapon of yours extremely *sui generis (one of its kind)*. Dream interpretation was so special to Joseph alone that he was the only option in the whole of Egypt, when Pharaoh had dream crisis. That is where God is taking you to. To be of value in the nations - in the valley and on the mountain top. To get there be eager to be more than you are right now. Where is your hunger?

Again you wonder how Joseph was able to dish out commands in a land that is not his father's. I believe you know Israel and Egypt linguistic proximity is not near. How, then, was he able to speak the Egyptian tongue? This isn't a mystery. It wasn't the heavenly tongue. Joseph added value to himself. He fed well. He knew there was more to just having a dream of purpose. He added virtue to his faith. Are you envisioning to be a great diplomat? You will be at a great degree of importance to be versed in many tongues of nations.

Daniel also wasn't exempted in this wise. Daniel chapter 1 verse 4 records that he and his friends, "*…had ability in them to stand in the king's palace, and whom they might teach the literature and the language of the Chaldeans*".

If Joseph, Daniel and his friends had not feed and developed capacity to bear this task ahead by learning the language beyond Hebrew, they might never be able to sustain their success. Joseph might be able to govern Egypt. While the chances of Daniel doing exploit among the Chaldeans might be slim.

2. Virtue

Another twin nutrient you wouldn't miss is virtue. You must strive to be man of virtue. Virtues are those behaviors which are in accordance with moral principles. Those behaviors or thought that conform to the parameters of morality. You might simply want to say virtues are *good moral conduct*. A man of value but not of virtue is a man with a stinking wound. No wonder the Holy Spirit exhorts through Peter that we should *add to our faith virtues*. What it means is that you should be a man of attestable character.

Character, generally, are like gaseous substance. They either choke you or move you. Virtues are like fragrance that moves a man towards the carrier, while bad character are like odor that chokes a man away from the host. Take it and don't leave it that what makes a Christian a winning man is not a function himself alone but of others. Many at times, you get cherished and favored by a man just because he likes your character. Virtues are pheromone of favorable visitations. The very day you begin to cultivate attributes that are uncalled for, you begin to lose taste in the tongue of men. *"If a salt loses its own savor, of what good is it again? But to be trodden under the foot of men."*

Many mighty men with admirable vision had fallen because they lack good moral conduct. King Nebuchadnezzar, though a heathen king, understood this principle. He ordered that not only skillful, intelligent or competent men be brought to serve him, but they must be of a noble descent. The most important qualification was that they must be of Noble blood. The Nobles are known to be people whose thoughts and behavior are in accordance with strictures of morality. This virtue alone was able to keep Daniel's success story going.

3. Valor

Human life is in phases. And with each phase comes new and greater challenges. It's more like a Mario game. Each level is difficult than the other. You would crash down later on in life if you aren't gallant enough. You must exercise the muscles of your mind to be able to carry the burden of the next phase and face its challenges. A man of valor is a man whose mind is strengthened towards danger. When you have valor, you possess that quality which enables you to encounter danger with firmness. It is synonymous to Bravery, courage, prowess and intrepidity.

Because a soldier knows that *there is more* to just being a soldier, he would exercise his mind in a way that he would be fearless on the battlefield. There is more to being called nice and honorable names. Merit the title people give to you.

Companies who are challenged with bankruptcy had gone sold out because they are headed by CEOs that are matured enough in their mind to stand the test of difficult time.

Age doesn't determine whether you are courageous or not. Even though, Nehemiah was matured in mind enough to stand the challenges from Sanballat and Tobiah.

I would like to refresh the success story of David in your mind. In Samuel's pursuit to look for a king to replace Saul, *one of the servants answered and said, look, I have seen a son of Jesse the Bethlehemite, who is skillful in playing, a mighty man of VALOR, a man of war, prudent in speech, and a handsome person; and the lord is with him.* 1 Samuel 16:18 (NKJV)

This is an answer to the question why David was able to challenge and conquer Goliath, the Philistine Giant. He was a man of valor right from the beginning of his success story where he was still fighting lions in the wilderness. He could advance beyond the status quo of killing lions with bear hands to killing Nephilim with mere stone because he knew there was more to his vision. My dear brother, would leave the stage of lion-killer to Goliath-slayer, and exhibit a show of gallantry.

COMPLACENCY

I have come to comprehend that what makes people lose hunger to feed their vision is because they are okay where they are. Why wouldn't you eat when your stomach can accommodate more than you have eaten?

Elijah couldn't let God continue with the plot of his success over the heathen because he grew complacent with what he has and what he had been given. The only thing you can get from your comfort zone is nothing but death.

Develop this unsatisfactory hunger for your destiny. Your belly can stomach it. If the bible says out of your belly shall flow rivers of living water. Not even ponds or stream. It says rivers. What would you want to settle for a glass of water?

DILIGENCE

"Therefore, Brethren, be all the more diligent to make your calling and election sure. For if you do these things, you will never stumble."

- 2 Peter 1 :10 (IKJV)

To stay successful and keep treading on the path of fulfillment, you must be diligent. Peter was intentional enough to say without mincing words that believers are not only to be diligent but to be *the more diligent.* The very day you feel you have been diligent enough, your success rate begins to diminish. The call to Christianity isn't a call to mediocrity or slothfulness.

The exhortation to the church from Peter to be diligent was not towards the things outside the will of God. He knew it's very well possible to be diligent towards negativity. But what you should channel your diligence towards is the surety of your calling – not just your calling. Your vision is your calling. To secured and advance beyond that winning status of that vision, you must remain diligent.

How much the scripture frowns at laziness and slackness! God conceived a vision in the beginning to create the heavens and the earth. He birthed this by diligence. He (God) worked before he rested, not otherwise. He was not relenting until he nurtured that vision. Even till date, God is still diligent in creativity. He so much admires diligence that it takes a diligent man to seek him rewardingly. So, if God isn't slack towards His dealing, why then should you, His son, be slack?

Failure to be diligent has made many men who were once shinning bright like the stars to become dim. There is no fuel of diligence to keep the flame of progress burning.

Have you stumbled on the road of success? Check, it might be your failure to be diligent towards your purpose. Have you toyed with your vision? God said *if you do these things, one of which is to be diligent, you will never stumble again on the path of success.*

Cultivate the attitude of Oliver Twist who never wants enough. Always the more.

COMPARISON

Myles Munroe, defining success, said that *"Success is not a comparison of what we have done with what others have done."* It is simply comparing what you are doing or have done to what you ought to have done. The equilibrium of success is reached when what you are doing is equal to what you ought to have done. You begin to decline the very moment you start to compare your progress or harvest with that of others.

God, who is the author and finisher of our success story, has made each person's story distinct and unique. Any effort to compare it with others' will definitely lead to failure.

The Israelites were enjoying their Divine-centered reign (what modern politics might call theocracy) under God, until they grew jealous of other nations and demand for a reign under a mortal man. Why would you grow jealous of others?

If you must continue to scale the utmost height, you must have this registered in the chambers of your heart that you are UNIQUE. Write it somewhere today. What is poisonous to the human metabolism might not be poisonous to the animals. Have you wondered why? Simply put, their make-up is different. They are unique in their own making. When comparison comes knocking at the door of your heart, bid it no welcome.

Know this and know peace that the success pace of everyone isn't equal. Just keep going on your own lane and at your own speed. I once watched a short video clip of two gold miners mining underground. Frequently, miner A keeps mining gold and kept offloading them at the surface. While miner B didn't. at a time where miner A had gone up the surface to offload his gold, miner B left is apportioned side and went digging that of A. unknown to him, there were no more gold on that side.

Whereas, if he had kept digging, he would have started reaping the good of his labor. After digging on the side of A for a while without getting in touch with any gold. He got frustrated and gave up working. This is the perfect scenario for most people. They have their mission frustrated because they have been so busy comparing ourselves with others that we lost touch of ours. Success isn't by comparison of what others have done to what you have done.

Ok, so you would understand better. The creation of plants is by kinds. They all have different seasons of harvest. The annuals are there. Some are biennial, while some are perennial in their seasons. Maize, for instance, is an annual crop which grows within 110 to 120days; it takes a standard size apple up to 8 years to bear its own fruit. Even, the dwarf apple specie takes not less than 2 to 3 years to bear fruit. It would communicate no sense if the Apple tree compares itself to the maize. "Why haven't I grown my seeds by now?" It wouldn't ask. It would wait for its own season.

The truth is that both plants are evidently growing. But the time of a fuller manifestation is different. Many had lost their appetite for more of progress in their vision because they had gotten distracted by the manifestation of others vision. No wonder, many crash at the peak of their endeavors.

BAD COUNSEL AND COMPANY

The nation of Israel was enjoying the government of a wise and wealthy king. A king who God *gave wisdom and understanding and largeness of heart, as the sand that is on the seashore.* He was rich in counsel, in gold and in silver. His reign was peaceful and successful UNTIL he married women from the nations God had forbade him to marry from. Solomon began to lose touch with his vision the moment he began to marry strange women. The right king got the wrong companion. Have you ever seen a mosquito feed a bloodless body before? Of course not. Sometime in a bid to kill our booming and fresh vision, the devil orchestrates blood-sucking friends or relatives to suck the life out of our sound vision. That is why you would see a man who had been successful become a failure. Check the company he keeps.

Such counsel may not necessarily come directly from men. You can fetch counsel from the well of the books you read. The books you feed on would immensely define the shape your vision would take whether it would fit in the next phase of your life. Haven't you seen people who went wild after consuming morsels of infected counsels from books that corrupted their destiny? The shape of your vision is meticulously carved that not all knowledge can fit in.

Getting your light covered with wrong counsel from the wrong company is something you wouldn't want to create room for. It could ruin a vision you have been building for a lifetime. Haven't you seen leaders of nation who were once prosperous in their call to leadership but suddenly got their attention turned otherwise? Most are resultants of wrong counsel or company.

Give little access to people in your success story. Not everyone is a cast in the play of your endeavor. Learn to scrutinize every advice you take from people. Be meticulous of the company you keep if you want to stay successful.

You wouldn't want to joke with the progression of your success.

Listen, it could take years or even decades to build something, but it doesn't take more than a minute to get it destroyed. I'm sure you must have been familiar with the famous 9-11 incident at the World Trade Center. It took four solid years for the Twin Tower of the World Trade Organization to be built. As a matter of fact, the second tower (2 WTC [SOUTH], as at then, was the tallest building in the world. These towers were destroyed by the Al-Qaeda terrorist group on the eleventh of September 2001, in couple of minutes. A single corrupt counsel could turn a booming vision to ruin. It's lethal than a terrorist bomb.

King Solomon's successor to the throne didn't escape being a victim of finding himself in a bad counsel-infested environment. He was so gullible to log into this software that it caused him the division of his vision.

Actually, you can't escape proposals of advices that are backed to be good. It would take your resilience to give no little access for them. This is more reason why you must be discerning. God take great delight in Christians who would stand their ground and preserve their success by forging ahead, void of leeches of bad counsel.

FOLLOWING FULLY

"Now give me this hill country that the lord promised me that day."

- Joshua 14:12a

The greatest secret of all, in savaging your journey to success, is to follow Jesus fully. Jesus on his venture to fulfil destiny told his disciples, *"follow me and I will make you fishers of men."* He met Levi by the publican office. Living a frustrated life. He met Peter and Andrew casting a net into the sea. Struggle to fulfill purpose that wasn't theirs. But he gave them hope. Jesus met all his disciples doing the wrong assignment. What would have happened, if they hadn't followed Jesus? Would they have remained failures? Yes.

The fact is that many plane of destiny comes crashing after a while because, it wasn't the right journey at first. Perhaps, it's the right journey but the wrong route. So, tell me "if *the foundation is destroyed, what shall the righteous do?*"

So don't start your quest for success outside of Christ. You can do nothing without Christ, that's what He says in John 15.

Joseph was following Jesus, when he told Potiphar's wife that he wouldn't lie with her. He had the company and consciousness of Christ on the road to success, which is why his success story wasn't cut short. Failure would have come beckoning if Joseph hadn't made Jesus his driver.

Give men little access to your assignment, but give Christ all access. Don't password your life to Christ. Let Him have unrestricted access. He would intervene in your course and you will never get disappointed. Fling the door opened always for Him to come in.

The disciples were progressing their call to preach the gospel and heal the sick. They were crossing to the other side. But they never dare leave Jesus out. He was in the boat with them all along. So, when the storm that comes with crossing on to the next level came. They were able to quiet the storm, because they had Jesus as their company and the captain of their endeavors.

Many get their boat of purpose and assignment swallowed up in the storm of life, because they tried to paddle the canoe without Jesus. That's not the example of a man who wants to be successful. There is no hard and fast rule, challenges will come in form of discouragement, threat and even bankruptcy, but what can make you scale through is the Jesus you have. His name and nature is Emmanuel. He came for you, because you can't do it allow. Journey on the aisle of success with Him.

CHAPTER 9

IN PURSUIT OF EXCELLENCE

Brian Harbor, in *Rising above the Crowd*, said *"success means being the best. Excellence means being your best. Success, to many, means being better than everyone else. Excellence means being better tomorrow that you were yesterday. Success means exceeding the achievements of other people. Excellence means matching your practice with your potential."*

We are about to get really personal about success more than we were at the previous chapter. Now the hunger to do more has been revived in you. But I must tell you, to savage the pendants of success, you must have a drive. Everyone who are on the track of success are being motivated by one thing or the other. There is a single drive you should have as a Christian. It is the drive of excellence.

Excellence is the force that pulls you towards your best. God utmost craving is that you move in progression, whether forward or upward, but never downward or backward. You should never remain where you were yesterday. That is progression.

Oh! I remember the words of an old friend of mine that says champions are goers. They aren't stayers. They quest in the forward locomotion. Why should you be different? As I have mentioned earlier in this book, Christians aren't mediocre. We are champions.

After God had gone six days into the creation, he created living creatures. The bible records in Genesis chapter 1:25,

*"And God made the beast of the earth after his kind, and the cattle after their kind, everything that creepeth upon the earth after his kind: AND GOD SAW THAT IT WAS GOOD." (*KJV)

You see that? God was good in his work of art. Yet, he didn't stop there. He forged ahead. You must not be different. Being just good would pay you a bit. So, He created man, as the caretaker of the beautifully fashioned Garden of Eden. After He had done this, it says in verse 31 that,

"And God saw everything that he had made, and behold, IT WAS VERY GOOD. And the evening and the morning were the sixth day."

How awesome God was, is and will be forever. God didn't halt at being *good*. He advanced towards *very good*. God was in pursuit of something, and that is EXCELLENCE. You should move beyond the parameter of your good to your very good; in your profession, school, and work and even ministry. The icy of the whole creation was that, still, God didn't put a full stop at being *very good.* He observed that *it is not good that man should be alone.*

So, he created an extension of man, a helpmate – Eve. God didn't stop until *all things were wonderfully made*. That is the model you should follow. The model in pursuit of excellence. In this chapter, I'm going to show you how key excellence is to the sustainability of success. After reading this, you're going to jolt for nothing else than excellence in the execution of your assignment and vision.

WHAT EXCELLENCE IS AND ISN'T

What then is excellence? On an adventure to unravel the meaning of success, several persons had gone outside the confines of the mind of God to define excellence. In turn, this has led many on a wild goose chase. So you wouldn't want skip this part of this book. The understanding of a thing will determine to a great deal the amount of value you attach to it.

Actually, before I step ahead to tell you what excellence is not and what excellence is, I wouldn't want to sacrifice telling you two vitals things.

Number 1: Success, though synonymously used with excellence, isn't the same with excellence.

Let's say you are in a school. The classes you attend, the assignment you attempt, the test you write and the examinations you sit for are all being done in a bid to qualify you for a degree. That's the force. The aim of pursuing your degree is what determines your attitude towards your studies – whether negative or positive. The evidence you can show to prove that you passed through a school would be the degree or certificate you obtain. If you told me, "I'm a Harvard School graduate," what would I say? "Show me you certificate to prove that".

Now, look, this is what I'm pulling at. Success is a school. Excellence is the degree - that which drives you on the corridors of success. You aren't qualified to be called a success until you have cultivated the attitude of pursuing excellence. You're a dropout from the school of success, if you lose your desire to always produce the best of you.

You can either fall into two categories in the school of success. Either you've dropped out due to results that aren't encouraging or you have decided to join the complacent gang. Perhaps you aren't doing enough. This book will draw you to the maximum elasticity of your potential. You can't settle for the ordinary.

Number 2: Excellence is a function of the spirit

Before I explain this, I would like you to consider the two scriptures below:

"Forasmuch as an EXCELLENT SPIRIT, and knowledge, and understanding, interpreting of dreams, and showing of hard sentences, and dissolving doubts, were found in the same Daniel..." Daniel 5:12 (KJV)

"Then this Daniel was preferred above the presidents and princes, because an EXCELLENT SPIRIT was in him; and the king sought to set him over the whole realm." Daniel 6:3 (KJV)

The spirit being made reference to is not the spirit of God. If you check the translation of that word *spirit*, it is pronounced *"roo'akh"* and it means the mind. So, that it was said that Daniel had an excellent spirit means he had an excellent human spirit – mind. Which means, on the seat of his emotions (mind) sat excellence. To be excellent, you must train your mind to love excellence. His central processing organ is engulfed with the aroma of excellence. I will tell you more about this later in this chapter.

Now to the essence of excellence. I would first like to draw out what excellence isn't for you.

- **Excellence isn't skills.**

Excellence isn't a skill but an attitude. Enza Artino said *"Attitude is the way of behaving, based on our inner motivations, personal values and aims."* While skills are *"those activities or capabilities we are able to do and deliver. They are what we learnt during our professional career."* Attitude is the readiness of the psyche to act or react in a certain way. Skill is the ability to do something that comes from training, experience or practice.

This is the reason I said earlier on that the abode of excellence stems from the human mind. Excellence is not imposed from without. It's from within. Do you know why I'm telling you this? So you can cultivate the attitude to pursue excellence. You can't get it in a day. You need to tend it. You can be an apprentice to be skillful, but you can't be an apprentice to be excellent. If you must have an excellence spirit, you must build it from the foundation of your mind.

Often, I see pastors pray for their members to go and excel. But I see the congregation doing nothing to pursue excellence. It could also be possible that you read this whole book embedded with treasures of wisdom and still remain on the average. This is because your mind must be willing to pursue excellence. It's not just about learning it. It's about loving it with your spirit. Wed your spirit with excellence so it might be called, just like Daniel, an excellent spirit.

- **Excellence doesn't come by chance**

You would be a mediocre forever, if you assume that excellence can come without work. Journey to the best of you isn't a chance game. There is nothing like "you can be excellent by luck."

Vince Lombardi, the notable head coach of the Green Bay Packers, once said that *"the only place success comes before work is in the dictionary."* It's going to be a white elephant project to pursue excellence without the virtue of hard work. To every good work comes a virtue. That of excellence is hard work. It's a perquisite.

- **Excellence isn't Perfection**

The last thing I would want to rid your mind off about excellence is to think that excellence is perfection. Don't misread that. Excellence is attained by pursuing perfection, but they are never the same. Most times, people get weary and can't advance in the school of success because they think excellence is perfection. Instead of just pushing towards better at that drawing of yours, don't throw away the pencil. Erase the figure and draw again and again.

The very day you think you have arrived at the junction of perfection, in your endeavor, your success story has lost the touch of excellence. Perfection isn't attainable, but if we chase perfection, we can catch excellence.

Excellence is doing little things in extraordinary ways. That imperfect endeavor of yours, carry on. Tends towards a more perfect version of it. That's an excellence spirit.

- **Excellence is being your best**

"The greatest enemy of progress is your last success; you could become so proud of what you've already accomplished that you stop moving ahead to what you can still accomplish."

In you is a lot of treasure and capacities God has deposited. You wouldn't want to settle for the less when you have abundance sealed in you. Majority of persons have only used 1% of their abilities. How sad it is for God to see.

People ask, "How can I get the best of me?" It's simple. Make God your audience. You have not been able to unleash your best because you have performed before men. Let me tell you. The praises of men could be deceptive at times. Some for the good reason. You get egged on so as not to feel bad at times. And you think you are doing your best. When you ride on the chariot of men's applause, eulogy and praises, it won't take you far. The speed of men's encouragement is super slow. It won't take you anywhere near excellence. Daniel didn't get flattered by the approval of Nebuchadnezzar. He didn't let his praises be his drive. The best of man is the least of God, but the best of God is the best of you. That was why he said "be perfect just as I am perfect." If you must be excellent, please God.

God will want you to be used to the full. He created you. Just think about the state of His heart if He is there sitting at the audience seat. Watching you using the least of you. A creature He has made for Himself. It pains to see. So, if you must experience excellence to savage your place in the school of success, make God your audience.

Truly, the definition of excellence to the secular world is being the best of others. But as a Christian, it's being the best of you. We aren't driven by competition.

This was a secret Daniel knew that made him had an excellent spirit. The secret of "God my audience." Even when asked by the king to interpret his dream, he must first ask from God his audience. He knew even a nod from God was able to promote him to the next phase in the school of success in pursuit of excellence.

- **Excellence is Quality above Quantity**

Don't forget this. Excellence is quality. Never quantity. The measure of an excellent enterprise is not in how much or how many. It is in how well. It doesn't really matter how much of assignment you do; it is a matter of how well you do them. So, as you pursue excellence, let the scale of the measurement be kilo-quality and not kilo-quantity.

In the school of success, if you are in the school of ministry, what qualifies and quantifies your ministerial excellence is not the number of your member; it is how impactful you're and they are to the world. Fine, quantity is good, but that doesn't determine success. Don't get deceived by it. As a matter of fact, most inventors made a lot of things, yet, they were mostly known for one thing.

If you were to do some shopping in the grocery store, would you prefer to buy a basket of rotten apple or you will just settle for ten good apples? The ten good ones, of course. In the market of life, don't opt for those items that are substandard but above standard.

That is why I love the bible. It says in Ecclesiastes 9 verse 10 that, "*whatever your hands to do, do it with your might;*" (NKJV) you see that? It could be a single assignment the lord is committing in your hands. Just do it with all your might. Craving for the best quality. Reinhard Bonnke was an evangelist sent to the African nation, just like Paul was sent to the Gentiles, yet he was excellent in that part of the world, because he did it to the best.

Make sure what you offer to the world is quality enough. Because, nobody is remembered for quantity but quality living.

EXCELLENCE IS BEING EXTRAORDINARY

To be excellent means to be beyond the ordinary. You wouldn't want to be ordinary and successful at the same time. Men who had their names written in the sand of time were men who did extraordinary things. The life of an excellent being is such life lived beyond boundaries and expectation. Boundaries aren't prisons; they are the standard set by men.

There was a standard and version of righteousness laid in the bible by men. But Christ, frowning at that said, *"...except your righteousness shall exceed the righteousness of the scribes and Pharisees, ye shall in no case, enter into the kingdom of heaven."* Matthew 5:50 (KJV)

There is also a standard of excellence that the world has orchestrated, in a bid to limit the best of you. To hinder your progress in the journey to success. I would like to put that Matthew 5:20 like this: *"Except your endeavor exceed the standard of the world. You will never near the corridor of success."*

Excellence wouldn't want its pursuer be imprisoned in the boundaries of men's record.

Get people wowed by your actions. It would be bad if they say *"of course, he should be able to do that. Nothing special."* Excellence is getting people's mouth wide open at your positive abnormality.

People were wowed to see Jesus teaching with authority, that they asked "isn't this Jesus, the carpenter. The son of the carpenter?" They were astonished at His extra-ordinary living.

The expectation of the Israelite was not towards anybody rescuing them from the giant. But David lived above that expectation. He took up that challenge. He was extraordinary. *Is he not the son of Jesse? Isn't he the little shepherd boy?* I'm sure those were the questions running through many minds that day. Yet he lived beyond the boundaries.

Live above your age and background. Whether you came from a poor background shouldn't deny you of your share of the excellent spirit.

DOSES FOR EXCELLENCE

1. RENEWAL OF THE MIND

The Oxford Advanced Learner's Dictionary, defined the word *renew* to mean *"begin something after it or was interrupted."* It also means to restore; to change. The journey to excellence starts from the mind. Because until your mind changes, nothing changes.

The bible says in Romans 12 verse 2 that, *"...be ye not conformed to this world this world: but be ye transformed by the renewing of your mind, that ye may prove what is that good, and acceptable and perfect, will of God."* (KJV)

I would have you know that God didn't fashion you in a way that you won't thirst for excellence. But the world system is feeding a lot of believers with the wrong dish that cannot change their destiny. You have to restore that.

To begin to excel, first thing is to align your mindset. Excellence is a girl who is too jealous to share the seat of your emotions, thought and will with any other thing that would welcome its stay in your spirit. Get rid of friends like low self-esteem, complacency, lethargy etc.. You have a new friend now. They must leave. Make proper sanitation of your mind and welcome excellence.

As you would need a mop stick, broom or a cleaning tool to restore your room that's messed up back, you need the greatest tool of all to renew your mind. And that's the word of God. Make it your daily food. Imbibe the principle there. Go excel in God's way.

Also, you need to start to control your mind. People will come and tell you, you can't do it. The discouragement of men. Those past failures will keep haunting you. The mind is like a mirror. It reflects whatsoever you have heard or seen – whether ugly or beautiful. But you have control over your mind. Think on the good things. The bible says in Philippian 4:8 that *"whatsoever things are true, whatsoever things are honest, whatsoever things are just, whatsoever things are pure, whatsoever things are lovely, whatsoever things are of good report; if there be any praise, think on these things."* That's how you can tailor your mind towards excellence.

2. CREATE DESTINY RELATIONSHIP

The clue of this book is that you give "little" access to men to determine your destiny, but never give "no access". God has ordained to every man that must excel a destiny relationship. Destiny relationships are relationship bonds and sealed by covenant. This isn't blood covenants or any kind outside the purview of the mind of Christ. I mean agreement. Amos 3:3 says *can two walk together unless they agree?* It's not possible. Whatever company of relationship you keep, they must agree with your destiny. These kinds of friends are such kinds that stick closer than a brother. You need them.

A perfect portrait of a destiny relationship in the scripture is that of David and Jonathan. The agreement of Jonathan with the destiny of David was so complementary that Jonathan Saul told David Jesse that *"whatever your soul desires, I will do it for you"* 1 Samuel 20:4(IKJV). You need that kind of relationship. God has raised men who will serve as a step for Him to lift us up to greatness. It's quite possible that David may never become the successor to Saul, if he didn't have a friend like Jonathan. Because he saved him many times from the fiery dart of his father.

In days like this, you don't really need a friend who will strip himself of his robe, armor, even his sword and his bow and his belt, but rather you need friends who can sacrifice their lives for you. Who can give up their time, energy, and resources for you.

Do you know Jesus had the seventy? He had the twelve, he had the three and even the one. That shows how much you need to know that certain person matters at certain stage in life. He was able to excel.

I would be doing you much harm than good to tell you you don't need men. No one is an island. Don't be a Robinson Crusoe. If you lack destiny relationship, pray to God to help fix you to who will help your adventure to excellence. Learn from David; learn from Jesus.

3. GRACE FACTOR IN EXCELLENCE

"May the grace of the Lord Jesus Christ, and the love of God, and the fellowship of the Holy Spirit be with you all." (2 Corinthians 13:14)

Did you ever asked why Paul the apostle always prayed for grace to all the people and churches whom he wrote his epistles to? The impact of grace over a man's life is immeasurable. I tell you. Above all things, grace will make you excel. In grace you will even find excellence.

Grace singles you out. And that is, of course, among all the nobles. Daniel became a great politician. Grace made him have an excellent spirit. Sometimes your strength will fail you, because by strength shall no man prevail. Jesus is the pioneer of this grace. He introduced grace when He came to the earth. So to receive grace, you need to stick with Him. Be consistent in your relationship with Him. Grace can grant you Godspeed.

But can I strike this note that the emergency and availability of grace isn't a call to idleness? Look at what the Bible says in Titus 2:11-14

"For the grace of God that brings salvation has appeared to all men, teaching us that, denying ungodliness and worldly lusts, we should live soberly, righteously, and godly in the present age, looking for the blessed hope and glorious appearing of our great God and Savior Jesus Christ, who gave Himself for us, that He might redeem us from every lawless deed and purify for Himself His own special people, zealous for good works." (NKJV)

One of the things grace will come to do in your life is to help you excel, and in doing that, it teaches you to deny ungodliness. What is ungodliness? Well, ungodliness could mean sin and every unrighteousness. But ungodliness could also mean anything, practice or habit that is not glorifying God and His work. So, you see, not living a life up to the standard of God. A life below standard is ungodly because it's not God's kind of thing; it's not His nature.

To wrap this up here, let me dish out some didactic lessons from the story of a great violinist by the name Nicolo Paganini.

Nicolo Paganini was invited to perform to a great audience. Just like being surrounded with a great cloud of witnesses watching with full eagerness to see what you would play with your God-given powerful weapon. As a figure who was in pursuit of excellence, Paganini decided to play a difficult and extraordinary piece. He was a man who walked in the path of living above human expectation.

He wasn't alone in this performance, as he had a full orchestra surrounding him. Everyone was expectant and ready for Paganini to serve them his quality entertainment. As expected, he started to play his violin in a melodious way. Unexpectedly, a string snapped from his guitar, living the guitar with only three strings. Paganini didn't stop; he improvised in his playing full of dexterity. After a while, more hurdle came as three more strings snapped from the violin. Left with one string, Paganini managed to play the difficult piece to the last note. He wowed everyone.

The gigantic audience stood to their feet as they shouted "bravo, bravo!" But Paganini wasn't lost in the ocean of their ovations. There was one more thing to do, which was practically impossible with a single string. Finishing the note was the least boundary the audience had set for him. At least he had done marvelously well enough. It was okay to stop right there. But Nicolo's view was different. He waved the audience to sit down. He was going to okay the encore. No way! Paganini played the final piece on the single-stringed Stradivarius beneath his chin. He hit the nail on the head. One of the greatest performances in the history of Italy. There is no definition that can be given to Nicolo Paganini's performance that day, but say, "It's EXCELLENT".

CHAPTER 10

THE LEGACY

"One generation shall commend your works to another, and shall declare your mighty acts."

- Psalm 145:4

Through the previous chapters of this book, you have been exposed to the importance of catching a vision and running with a God-given vision to achieve purpose. However, in this last chapter, I would be pointing your attention to an important aspect of the vision process. I will be talking about how important it is to have a vision that lives on as your legacy after you leave this earth.

Let's start with something simple: take a moment to think deep and tell me what these companies have in common: LVMH (Louis Vuitton), Walmart, Volkswagen and Ford— what are some of the guesses that run through your mind? I can guess one: all these companies are successful companies. Another guess might be that all of these companies are more than 5o years old.

Maybe you might also guess that every company there has consistently built their level of quality and consumer satisfaction over the years. Although all these are true, that's not the only thing they have in common. One of the most tremendous things about all these companies is that they are family businesses. They've been passed as legacy through a certain bloodline till today.

Let's take Louis Vuitton for instance. It was founded by a poor 16-year old boy after he travelled from his village to Paris and saw the great need for luxury and exquisite trucks that people can use in their daily life. However, when he died, the company did not die; it became a family legacy and today it is the second most valuable fashion brand in the world. As a matter of fact, its current CEO is the one of the five richest men in the world!

According to the Merriam Webster's dictionary, a legacy is something transmitted by or received from an ancestor or predecessor from the past. If you look closely at the way through which God reveals Himself to men, you will know that He is interested in legacies. He did not invite Joshua up to Sinai for another law, neither did He take Solomon through a Goliath. What God does is to reveal Himself to certain men and have them pass these experiences as a legacy to the upcoming generations.

In the Bible verse quoted above, you will see the way God loves things to be: a generation will reveal your works to upcoming generations. No wonder Peter could so passionately talk about the dealings God had with Moses and Paul could clearly speak of the fathers of faith. These stories have become legacies among the Israelites; it doesn't matter if Peter and Moses are almost 4,000 years apart, the legacy lives on.

You will agree with me that one of the greatest things God ever gave to men was the Bible. One of the most interesting thing about the Bible is that although the periods and times in which the writers lived in was different and their level of sophistication was different, they wrote almost the same subject matter. You could see the level of continuity in the narratives of the Bible and the agreement. This was achievable, as it was the Spirit of God that inspired all the writers. But this wouldn't have been possible if they had not learnt to relate with God. In Jewish societies, the stories of God's greatness have continuously being told, so much so that, God is the first heritage passed to a Jewish child. Which is why no matter how far apart they are, they can still write the same thing through the inspiration of God.

This same approach is what you must apply to your vision. You see, it is easy to have a vision and run with it alone but it is more difficult to make others understand the vision and run with it. However, a vision you carry and execute alone will die with you. If all you do with your time on earth is to chase a vision without bringing other people into it, you can be sure such a vision will die with you.

Such was the case of Eli the priest. He saw how the life of his children was becoming unlike God and His word but he just let it lie. And that was almost the end of His lineage on priesthood, if not for the grace of God. When you get a vision from God, it is important you raise replaceable sons and daughters who will see the light in what you are doing and shed this light over all the nations.

The question that rises then is this: how can one raise children that will carry one's vision as legacies? Is it only the children one gives birth to biologically that should run one's vision? Is it only people that got to know the Lord through someone? Well, the answer is simple: it is not only your biological sons or the people you brought to the Lord; it is as many as all who believe in the vision and can run with it.

Thankfully, the Bible does not leave us in the dark as touching the issue of legacies. Instead, it gives us the stories and experiences of patriarchs and matriarchs to learn from. This great cloud of witness are people who have lived and left a legacy that endured through space and time. Trying to generate a comprehensive list of these people will be exhausting, but we don't need a list. Do we?

Definitely not! We only need to consider their lives and draw inspiration and insight from this cloud of witnesses that would prove as lights to us as we hope to have a vision that endures beyond our lifetime. Hence, I would be considering three biblical characters as cloud of witnesses that we all can learn from. We'll be considering Jesus, Moses and Paul.

CLOUDS OF WITNESSES

(THE BIBLICAL PATTERN OF LEGACY BUILDING)

The bible is filled with stories of men and women who did not only live a victorious life but also left a legacy for the ones after them to live a victorious life. They were people that lived right, fulfilled purpose and kept on living after they had passed on to glory because they left an enduring legacy on the earth. From the unending list of men who left an enduring legacy, I'll be discussing the life and legacy of Jesus, Paul and Moses.

1. The Life and Legacy of Jesus: In the history of mankind, Jesus Christ is the greatest that ever lived. It is mind-blowing to see how an individual can be so great and yet so humble. He is the son of God Who came to die for the sins of all human beings, yet He is still the Son of man who had the feelings and sensibilities of human beings. During His lifetime, He defiled history, science and philosophies by doing things that the mind of man was too frail to comprehend.

His teachings were so comprehensive and deep that the wise men of His days were confounded by such level of wisdom. His ministry was filled with miracles, signs and wonders. He did not only heal the sick and open the blind's eye; He also raised up the dead, walked on the water and did do many other things that had never been done prior to that time in the history of mankind. The most interesting part of Jesus ministry is not only in the things He did but in the power He gives others to do it.

He did not only heal the sick; He empowered His disciples to do such miracles and more. This is what He says in John 14:12-14 thus: "Most assuredly, I say to you, he who believes in Me, the works that **I do he will do also**, because I go to My Father. And whatever you ask in My name, that I will do, that the Father may be glorified in the Son. If you ask anything in My name, I will do it."

Jesus did not only teach or inspire all around Him at the time of his ministry on earth, but also he made sure that all He taught was retained for a greater purpose even after His departure. Jesus taught His disciples how to pray in Mathew 6:5-12 and other scriptural passages. He taught them how to preach in Mathew 10:6-26 and other scriptural references. Even after Jesus' departure, all He taught was established and built on greatly.

These things Jesus taught His disciples and the power He gave them to do all He did, and more, ensured that the life of Christ continued on earth, even after He had died. The pattern of legacy building that Jesus taught His disciples was concurrent. In that Jesus taught His disciples and left a legacy with them; His disciples too raised disciples and left a legacy with them; those disciples also had disciples they left legacy with and the circle continued.

2. The Life and Legacy of Moses: Moses was a significant character in the bible who was used by the Lord to transport the first God-written constitution to man. Although he was born in the land of slavery and grew up as Pharaoh's son, he caught a burden for God and his life was dedicated to the liberation of the Lord's people from the Land of slavery to the Promised Land. When the Lord called him, his assignments were laid out clearly: he was to lead the people of God from bondage to freedom.

After Moses had caught a vision for his life and defined his life's purpose, he started walking in it through the directions and guidance. But then, at several points on His journey to destiny fulfilment, there were several people that helped him achieve His purpose while he was alive and even after he died. Let's consider closely how Moses trained Joshua to become a re-placeable son unto himself in the Lord.

"Then the Lord said to Moses, 'write this for a memorial in the book **and recount it in the hearing of Joshua,** that I will utterly blot out the remembrance of Amalek from under heaven'" (Exodus 17:14). In this verse of the bible, the Lord informed Moses to keep a memorial and recount it in the hearing of Joshua; this is a form of disciple making. We would later discuss how disciple making is one of the ways to ensure that one's legacy lives on as we go on with this chapter.

Can you recall that when Moses was going to Mount Sinai, Joshua went with him to a point? Joshua was there with Moses at Sinai. He was sent by Moses for wars, for spying and other important things. Joshua understood the importance of Moses' vision and purpose; he understood the implication of what God had for Moses. This understanding made it easy for him to run with the vision of Moses and finally fulfil it.

Don't forget, God called Moses to go liberate his people from slavery and deliver them to the Promised Land. However, you will note that Moses was only able to fulfil a part of the vision God gave to him. He was able to lead the people from slavery but not to the Promised Land. At some points in Moses' ministry he and the people he led made a grave mistake that caused the Lord to be annoyed with them.

Although God said that most people in that generation will not get to the Promised Land, Joshua was made as an exception. He had been trained to lead the people after Moses, hence when Moses and other people in that generation died, it was easy for him to step into the position of leadership because he had been training for it. The concern of God at Moses' death was not "who shall we send, who will go for us?" His concern was how to equip Joshua to fulfil what Moses left undone. So, when Moses died, Joshua stepped in and was able to lead the people into the land of Canaan.

At times, a legacy is not just lessons we take from people's life but an inheritance of the visions and purposes of another person. As we have seen in the case of Moses and Joshua. If Moses had not made his vision and purpose clear to Joshua, he would not have been able to achieve it after his death.

3. The Life and Legacy of Paul: The last person we'll examine his life and legacy as a cloud of witness through which Christians can draw inspiration for their lives today is Paul. Almost every Christian is familiar with the religious fanatic who killed others as a means of service to God and how that man was transformed totally by just a single encounter with Jesus Christ. You will agree with me that Paul is one of the most popular characters in the bible.

His popularity comes from the tremendous success he had in his ministry. He wrote epistles, endured hardship, led many to the Lord, transformed lives, preached to pagans and heathen and also confronted the Roman Empire with the perfection of God's enduring truth. What a man! All these notwithstanding, one of the most inspiring things for me about the life and ministry of Paul is how he left a legacy to the upcoming generations.

The legacies of Paul can be seen in most of his epistles, but the most interesting of all are his epistles to Timothy. From these epistles, we see Paul teaching his son in the Lord Timothy relevant life lessons that will help him grow into the image of Christ and also function as a carrier of Paul's legacies.

Let me draw your attention to the introductory parts of Paul's first epistle to Timothy: "To Timothy, a **true son in the faith**; Grace, mercy and peace from God our father and Jesus Christ or Lord. As I urged you when I went into Macedonia- remain in Ephesus **that you may charge some that they teach no other doctrine**…" (1Timothy 1:2-3)

The first interesting thing I want you to note from the bible verses quoted above is the fact that Paul calls Timothy a true son in the faith. This means that Paul was responsible for his spiritual nurturing and upbringing. And here it is, another clue from our cloud of witnesses: the mystery of parenting. One of the ways to leave a legacy behind is to raise "true sons and daughters in the faith." Your children in the faith will surely carry on whatever it is the Lord has started with you even when you are no longer around.

A contemporary example we have is Daniel Kolenda who was nurtured to maturity in the faith by the great evangelist: Reinhard Bonnke. After Bonnke's demise, his vision of taking the gospel of Christ to all nations did not die; Kolenda is still actualizing that vision today. That is how powerful spiritual parenting can be.

Another thing you would note throughout the book of Timothy was that Paul consistently taught Timothy and instructed him of things to do and things to beware of. And this is another clue you must not sweep under the carpet. Consistent instruction! You must understand the people you intend to raise as bearers of legacy are separate from you. They have their own wills, ambition, life goals and at times, vision. Hence, there is a need for consistent instruction and relentless teaching to make the vision you carry form in them.

Having considered how some characters in the bible raised men that carried on their vision after their death, it is important you know that anyone, but not just anyone, can bear the weight of your vision with you. What do I mean by this? There's nobody that is not teachable, trainable or usable by God. However, you can't commit your vision to just any one.

There's no particular group of persons or people you can't train to carry on your vision. There's no group of persons around you that you can't target as prospective legacy bearers. They might be your immediate family, your colleagues, your friends, your converts or maybe some distant people who just get inspired by what they see in your life.

The questions that rise then are these: How can one identify and train people to run with their visions? How can one make their vision into a legacy for people who didn't conceive it? Well, there are different ways people do that but I'll be sharing with you three Bible-proven methods that can help you sell your vision to coming generations.

FINAL NOTE

BIBLICAL METHODS FOR ESTABLISHING A LASTING LEGACY

1. Discipleship: Discipleship is a biblical principle that can never be overemphasized. Simply put, it's the means through which a person (disciple) puts himself under another person (discipler) to learn the principles of becoming like Christ. It's important I warn you to not be deceived as others have been deceived. Discipleship is not an end in itself but a means to becoming. In the same vein, its end is not to make people become like you, but rather to make them become like Christ.

Christ is the end of discipleship and because the life of Christ is different from the kind of life we have been exposed to, it is a continuous process. In short, the more you become, the more you need to become. And this is a powerful tool for making people come into the vision the Lord has revealed to you. It has been mentioned earlier in this book that a God-given vision is enough to take the totality of your life.

Now I tell you, a God-given vision will always transcend your life. God is so vast that you can't finish Him. Hence, the vision you'll receive from Him will be so vast that your life would be just a dot in the paragraph God is writing with you. This is why it is important you raise disciples to become like Christ. You have embraced Christ and are becoming more like Him; it is therefore important that you bring over men to know God.

When God communicates a vision to a man, it does not normally end with that man. Rather, it transcends him into generations to come. God called Paul to ministry amongst the gentiles. Although he dedicated the whole of his life to it, he couldn't exhaust it. He still invested in disciples that continued the work when he was no longer here. In the same vein, Christ came to establish the life of God on earth. He lived and died but the vision transcended his earthly sojourn and still continues till today.

As you train them to become more like Christ, because the vision you received from the Lord is for the glory of His name, you'll notice that that vision will become a legacy for your disciples. It has been mentioned earlier how Joshua patiently followed Moses. He was a disciple and he came into the vision God had for the life of Moses, to take the people to the Promised Land and he succeeded.

Discipleship is a serious training program where a Christian loses his life for the life of Christ. Let's see what Christ says about it in Matthew 16:24, *"Then Jesus said to His disciples, if any man will follow me: let him deny himself, take up his cross and follow me."* In the words of the verse quoted above, Jesus spells out in clear terms the demands and costs of discipleship. One must first deny himself before he can follow.

As a disciple of Christ, to ask Him for a heaven-inspired vision is a form of self-denial. An average human basing has his own ambitions, his career goals and all... seeking God for a vision is a form of denying oneself, patterning one's life according to the received vision is a means of following Christ's leading because that was what He did with His life while on earth.

Given that you have denied yourself of your ambitions and have followed God's own vision for your life, you are a disciple; it is important that you raise other disciples who will understand what it means to receive a vision from God and run with it. It might seem unlikely, but many a times, your disciples will receive complimentary visions that will help push your vision on even when you're no longer here.

2. Mentorship: According to the Merriam Webster's dictionary, mentorship is defined as the influence, guidance or direction given by a mentor. Before I continue talking about what Mentorship is, it is important we understand who a mentor is. A mentor is a trusted counsellor or guide, a coach or tutor. Although discipleship often encompasses mentorship, the scope of mentorship is more streamlined. It is precise and specific as to the areas it affects in an individual's life.

Mentorship is defined by the guidance an individual gives to another individual as regards a specific aspect of life, a particular goal or a particular project. While discipleship is targeted at the total development of all areas of an individual's life, mentorship is directed at a particular aspect of one's life. One can have an academic mentor who knows nothing about their finances and has no influences on them. While a discipler knows something about every area of a disciple's life and guides him through it all. Although it is important you raise disciples as a Christian, the fact is that not everyone can be your disciple.

There are people that may not be able to pay the price of discipleship. They might not be ready to leave the totality of their lives and follow your teaching, but you can still tutor in a particular sphere of life. You can still be their mentor and offer guidance in a particular area of their life. Earlier in this book, this question was raised: what is in your hand?

Again, I ask you, what is in your hand? What is that thing you know how to do? What is that thing the Lord has put in your hands to draw men to Him? Use it well, let your light so shine that men would be attracted to the light of God in you. Whatever career path you find yourself in, there are people there who would see your light and get attracted to it.

These people can become your mentees; it is a good thing to share your vision with your mentees. If your mentees see your God-given talents, there is high tendency that they'll believe in it later and they might even become disciples on the long run. This was the case with such people like Joseph of Arimathea and Nicodemus. They were not close disciples of Jesus but they were people whom Jesus mentored through His teachings. And the Bible records that it was Joseph of Arimathea that provided where Jesus was buried.

The place of Mentorship can never be overemphasised in selling out your vision to people. If your life inspires someone and they let you know of it, let them know of your vision. If there is someone you tutor, coach or mentor, the fact that your vision has filled you to the brim will make it that you consciously or unconsciously transfer your vision to them. So far the vision can either be shared consciously or unconsciously, it yields more result that way.

Finally, asides discipleship and mentorship, another way by which you can affect lives so much so that they'll carry on your vision even when you leave is through strategic influencing. There are people that are neither your disciples nor mentors but are in your sphere of influence. Speak to them of your vision and purpose; let them see the beauty of it and they might as well run with it after they've been influenced by it.

BOOK SUMMARY

When we talk of vision, it's the mental picture of what one wants to achieve in life. This is basically defined by short- or long-term grounds. This picture must be vivid, clear, and intense in our minds to get the desired drive for stepping into the plane of success. Vision is a "turner" of dreams into mentally achievable feet. Make no mistake; vision isn't a vague wish, dream, or hope. When you have a vision, it brings energies and beauties of the future to your present, making you willing to sacrifice and let go of anything for the moment.

Conceiving a vision is the beginning and the most potent foundation to lay in the school of success. Dive in and look at the kind of persons or individuals you allow into your success plan. Not everybody will add to your vision or success story. Hence, your commitment level to people must be defined by how relevant they are to the fulfillment of your purpose and vision. We will define clutters here in relation to all the things/people who may hinder your effectiveness in the pursuit of the fulfillment of your vision.

Here, we also want to launch into the guide to achieving success and fulfilling your vision. What are the things to do to birth your vision? The place of getting a mentor or a motivator will be explored as well. Indeed not everyone can midwife our vision. Take notes and use your keys to open the door, and walk into the door, but keep in mind who you should allow to COME IN with you.

Angella

www.ingramcontent.com/pod-product-compliance
Lightning Source LLC
Chambersburg PA
CBHW071401210526
45465CB00001B/198